MY GRANDDAUGHTER HAS FLEAS!!

Other Cathy® Books From Andrews and McMeel

Why do the right words always come out of the wrong mouth?
A hand to hold, an opinion to reject
Thin thighs in thirty years
Wake me up when I'm a size 5
Men should come with instruction booklets
A mouthful of breath mints and no one to kiss
Another Saturday night of wild and reckless abandon

MY GRANDDAUGHTER HAS FLEAS!!

A Cathy® Collection

by Cathy Guisewite

Andrews and McMeel
A Universal Press Syndicate Company
Kansas City • New York

CATHY ® is syndicated internationally by Universal Press Syndicate.

ISBN: 0-8362-1855-8

Library of Congress Catalog Card Number: 89-84809

MY FRIENDS ALL HURRY HOME FROM WORK TO BE WITH THEIR HUSBANDS...THEY PLAN EVERY DAY AROUND SPENDING TIME WITH THEIR CHILDREN....
MILK

IT MAKES ME FEEL IT'S TIME TO MAKE SOME BIG CHANGES OF MY OWN, MOM. I THINK I'M FINALLY READY TO MAKE A REAL COMMITMENT.
MILK

OH, SWEETIE, YOU MEAN YOU'RE... YOU'RE... YOU'RE...
I'M GO-ING TO GET A DOG!

...MOM??
GO AWAY. I WANT TO BE ALONE WITH MY HAPPINESS.

CATHY, GETTING A DOG IS A HUGE RESPONSIBILITY.
I KNOW THAT, MOM.

HOW WILL YOU HAVE TIME TO FEED IT? HOW WILL YOU HAVE TIME TO TAKE IT OUTSIDE? HOW WILL YOU HAVE TIME TO TRAIN IT? HOW WILL YOU HAVE TIME TO TAKE IT TO THE VET? HOW WILL YOU HAVE TIME TO PLAY WITH IT?

DON'T WORRY, MOM!

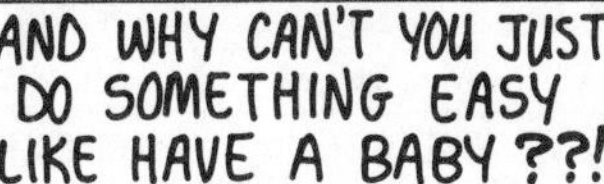
AND WHY CAN'T YOU JUST DO SOMETHING EASY LIKE HAVE A BABY??!

THE STAFF HERE AT THE HUMANE SOCIETY IS TRAINED TO BE ABLE TO TELL WHAT BREED OR BREEDS A PUPPY OR DOG MIGHT BE, AND WHAT HIS TEMPERAMENT AND SIZE WILL BE.
HUMANE SOCIETY
MR. LERNER
ADOPTION COUNSELOR

AFTER THAT, MOST PEOPLE JUST USUALLY GET A SPECIAL FEELING FROM ONE ANIMAL THAT LETS THEM KNOW IT'S THE RIGHT ONE FOR THEM TO ADOPT.
HUMANE SOCIETY

PICK ME.
PICK ME.
PICK ME.
PICK ME.
PICK ME.
PICK ME.
PICK ME.
PICK ME.
PICK ME.
PICK ME.
PICK ME.
PICK ME.
PICK ME.
PICK ME.

PLEASE
PLEASE.
PLEASE
PLEASE
PLEASE
PLEASE
PLEASE
PLEASE
PLEASE
PLEASE
PLEASE
PLEASE
PLEASE
PLEASE
I'M IN BIG TROUBLE.
HUMANE SOCIETY

THE HUMANE SOCIETY GETS A LOT OF GORGEOUS PUREBRED DOGS.
I NEED A BIGGER HOUSE.
HUMANE SOCIETY

WE HAVE DARLING PUPPIES, BEAUTIFUL MIXED BREEDS, AND LOVELY OLDER DOGS WHO ARE DESPERATE TO BE SOMEONE'S FRIEND.
I WILL MAKE A LOT OF MONEY AND BUY A HUGE HOUSE!
HUMANE SOCIETY

NO MATTER WHAT PEOPLE ARE LOOKING FOR, THEY FIND THE SAME SPECIAL THING HERE.
I'LL BUY AN ENORMOUS HOUSE WITH A HUGE YARD AND COME BACK TO RESCUE ALL THE ANIMALS!

THERE'S NOTHING LIKE ADDING TO YOUR FAMILY TO GIVE YOU A WHOLE NEW SENSE OF PURPOSE.
I WILL BUY AN ENTIRE CITY AND LET ALL THE DOGS MOVE IN!!!
HUMANE SOCIETY

SHE'S LOOKING AT ME. DON'T ACT TOO EXCITED. SHE'LL THINK I'M HIGH-STRUNG.

I CAN'T BELIEVE THAT PUPPY HASN'T BEEN TAKEN.
WELL, PEOPLE TEND TO TAKE ONLY THE CUTER DOGS. THIS ONE IS SO...
EXOTIC LOOKING.

SHE'LL MAKE A VERY NICE PET. SHE'S JUST SO.. YOU KNOW, SO...
PROFOUNDLY BEAUTIFUL.
HUMANE SOCIETY
ADOPTION COUNSELOR

I'M SURE YOU'LL GET ALONG FINE. COME TO THINK OF IT, YOU BOTH HAVE SORT OF THAT SAME....
CHOMP.
HUMANE SOCIETY
ADOPTION COUNSELOR

OW.
RAQUEL WELCH LOOK.
ADOPTION COUNSELOR

ANIMALS THAT HAVE BEEN ABAN-DONED ARE UNDERSTANDABLY NERVOUS ABOUT NEW PEOPLE.
ADOPTION COUNSELOR

YOU MAY WANT TO KEEP HER IN A NICE SECURE BOX UNTIL SHE GRADUALLY LEARNS TO START TRUSTING YOU AND HER NEW ENVIRONMENT.

OR YOU COULD JUST WEAR HER.
HUMANE

THIS IS THE BED WHERE YOU'LL SLEEP... THAT'S WHERE YOU'LL EAT... AND THERE'S THE LITTLE PLAY AREA WHERE YOU WILL KEEP ALL YOUR TOYS.

I AM NOT GOING TO TURN INTO ONE OF THOSE PEOPLE WHO LETS HER DOG SLOWLY TAKE OVER HER WHOLE LIFE!

IT'S SO MUCH MORE EFFICI-ENT TO JUST CAVE IN AFTER THE FIRST FIVE MINUTES.
CLICK.

IRVING, MEET MY PUPPY, ELECTRA.
ELECTRA?? YOU NAMED HER WITHOUT EVEN ASKING MY OPINION??

I DIDN'T WANT ANYONE'S OPINION ON THIS, IRVING.

THERE COMES A TIME IN A WOMAN'S LIFE WHEN SHE NEEDS TO JUST LOOK INWARD FOR THE ANSWERS!
I TYPED OUT A BATCH OF 200 MORE NAME SUGGESTIONS, SWEETIE!

CAN I HELP IT IF EVERY TIME I LOOK INWARD, MY MOTHER IS STANDING THERE WITH A LIST?

"ELECTRA" MEANS "DAZZLING, BRILLIANT BEAUTY." IT'S THE PERFECT NAME FOR MY PUPPY!
CATHY, SHE'S JUST A BROWN, SCRAGGLY MUTT.
BABY NAMES

IRVING, DON'T SAY THAT IN FRONT OF HER.
DOGS DON'T UNDERSTAND WHAT WE'RE SAYING. HA, HA!

LOOK AT HER. SHE LOOKS LIKE A "SCRUFFY" OR A "MUFFY" OR A "TRAMP"....

HE LOOKS LIKE A GEEK.

LET ME SEE ALL THE OTHER NAMES YOU HAVE MARKED FOR THE PUPPY IN YOUR BABY NAME BOOK, CATHY.
BABY NAMES

OH...UM, THOSE WEREN'T FOR HER.
WHO WERE THEY FOR?
FOR?? AHEM...NO ONE..UM..
WHY WOULD YOU HAVE BABY NAMES MARKED? WHY WOULD YOU EVEN HAVE A BABY NAME BOOK???

OH, NEVER MIND THE BABY NAME BOOK, IRVING. I BOUGHT IT FOR CATHY AND I'LL PUT IT AWAY.
THANK YOU, MOM.
BABY NAMES

SHE KEEPS IT RIGHT HERE IN HER SECRET DRAWER NEXT TO HER FILE ON BRIDAL PARTY PLACE SETTINGS!!
BABY NAMES

IT'S NORMAL FOR WOMEN CATHY'S AGE TO TRANSFER CERTAIN MATERNAL URGES ONTO A PET.
WE NEED TO ACT SUPPORTIVE OF HER DECISION TO GET A DOG, BUT ALSO REMIND HER THAT A DOG IS NO SUBSTITUTE FOR A REAL FAMILY. A DOG IS WON-DERFUL, BUT IT'S JUST A DOG. A CANINE. AN ANIMAL. A PET.

COME TO GRAND-MA!!
MOM'S FINALLY FLIPPED.
I KNOW, CATHY.

...AND GRANDPA'S GOING TO GET SOME PICTURES OF IT!!

SOME COUPLES DEAL WITH EVERY ISSUE THE SECOND IT COMES UP.
THAT HURT ME, DON.
LET'S TALK ABOUT IT, PAM.

SOME COUPLES LET LITTLE PROBLEMS ACCUMULATE UNTIL THEY MERIT A BIG DISCUSSION.
SOME THINGS ARE BOTHERING ME, KAREN.
WE'LL WORK THROUGH THEM TOGETHER, JOE.

SOME COUPLES NEVER ACTUALLY DEAL WITH THE INDIVIDUAL ISSUES, PREFERRING TO LET THEM KEEP HEAPING UP UNTIL THE FULL RANGE OF EMOTION CAN BE EXPRESSED.

THE "BURNING-THE-IN-BASKET" APPROACH TO PROBLEM-SOLVING.

YOU MAKE ME SICK!!!

PBLLLTTT!!!

"WHAT'S WRONG WITH YOU?"
"WHY CAN'T YOU COMMUNICATE?"
"WHEN ARE YOU GOING TO SHAPE UP?"
COLA
Make Love Work

"THESE ARE ABSTRACT QUESTIONS THAT DO NOTHING TO IMPROVE A RELATIONSHIP."
COLA
Make Love Work

"TO MAKE POSITIVE, HARMONIOUS CHANGES, PEOPLE MUST LEARN TO MAKE SPECIFIC COMMENTS THAT CAN BE ACTED UPON!"
COLA

WHY DON'T YOU THROW OUT THAT STUPID BOOK?
WHERE ARE ALL THE GOOD MEN?

A LOT OF COUPLES DON'T TALK ABOUT FEELINGS JUST BECAUSE THEY DREAD STARTING SOME LONG, EMOTIONAL CONFRONTATION, IRVING.

SO, THIS IS A TIMER. IF WE JUST SPEND FIVE MINUTES A WEEK DISCUSSING HOW WE FEEL, IMAGINE HOW WE COULD ENRICH OUR RELATIONSHIP!

WE MIGHT EVEN START LOOKING FORWARD TO IT.... FIVE LITTLE MINUTES A WEEK FOR US TO BE TOTALLY HONEST ABOUT EVERY HOPE, FEAR, ANXIETY, FRUSTRATION.....

BING!
TIME'S UP.
THANK HEAVENS.

I KNEW YOU'D BE LATE FOR THIS PARTY IF YOU STOPPED TO PLAY RACQUETBALL AFTER WORK, IRVING.
THE SET JUST RAN LONG, CATHY.

I TOLD YOU YOU'D BE LATE.
OK. I WAS LATE.
I PREDICTED YOU'D BE LATE! I WAS SURE YOU'D BE LATE!
FINE. YOU WERE RIGHT.

I KNEW AT 9:00 THIS MORNING THAT YOU'D BE LATE TONIGHT!
FINE! YOU WERE RIGHT! YOU WIN!! NOW CAN WE DROP IT ?!!

IT ISN'T ENOUGH TO WIN. I WANT THE AWARDS CEREMONY.

YOU LOOK GREAT, CATHY!
GREAT?? HAH! THIS IS A DUMPY OLD SWEATSUIT! I LOOK LIKE AN EGGPLANT!

...NO. WAIT... THAT WAS HORRIBLE! I NOT ONLY POINTED OUT MY OWN FLAWS, BUT INSULTED YOUR JUDGMENT.

JUST START OVER, IRVING. COME IN AGAIN AND I'LL BE A MODEL OF POSITIVE SUPPORT!

YOU LOOK LIKE AN EGGPLANT.
I LOVE YOUR REPULSIVE SENSE OF HUMOR.

WAAHH!!
TURN THE CAR AROUND, LUKE.

WE CAN'T GO ON VACATION WITHOUT OUR BABY, LUKE!! WE'RE 35 MILES AWAY AND I CAN STILL HEAR HER SCREAMING! LUKE... PLEASE!

WAAHH!!

THAT'S YOUR VOICE, ANDREA.
OH.

IS LITTLE ZENITH STILL SHRIEKING AND SOBBING FOR HER MOMMY, CATHY ?
NO, ANDREA. SHE HASN'T CRIED AT ALL.
HONE

IS SHE THROWING TEMPER TANTRUMS ABOUT HER FOOD BECAUSE IT'S NOT HOW MOMMY MAKES IT ?
NO. SHE SEEMS PER-FECTLY HAPPY.
PHON

SHE'S PER-FECTLY HAPPY ?
SHE'S HAVING A GREAT TIME, ANDREA ! JUST RELAX AND ENJOY YOUR SPECIAL VACATION WITH YOUR HUSBAND !
PHON

DON'T TOUCH ME !!
PHONE

YOU'D BETTER BABY-PROOF THIS ROOM BEFORE YOU PUT ZENITH DOWN, CATHY.
I DON'T BELIEVE IN BABY-PROOFING, MOM.

A CHILD IS PERFECTLY ABLE TO RESPECT AN ADULT ENVI-RONMENT IF YOU JUST TAKE A FEW MINUTES TO CLARIFY HER BOUNDARIES.

SMASH
BAM BAM
RIP
WAD
CHOMP
SHRED
SPLAT
TRAMPLE
STUFF
BOUNCE

ALL OF THAT WAS "NO."

ZENITH, PLEASE TAKE A NAP SO I CAN GET SOMETHING DONE ! PLEASE... I HAVE TO FIX DINNER, DO THE LAUNDRY, CLEAN THE HOUSE, PAY BILLS...
EEYAA !

JUST TAKE A NAP ! JUST GO TO SLEEP ! I'M BEGGING YOU, ZENITH ! TAKE A NAP ! I CAN'T DO ANYTHING UNTIL YOU...
EEYAA !

Z Z
Z Z

EEEYAAA !
I MISSED IT !!

BA!
NO, ZENITH. YOUR MOMMY SAID NO TV UNTIL WE PRACTICE YOUR NUMBERS.
Baby's First Numbers

BA BA BA!
SEE THE FUNNY NUMBER BOOK? WON'T IT BE FUN TO LEARN ABOUT NUMBERS?

BA!

ZENITH: 483.
AUNT CATHY: ZILCH.

...OH, A BABY! LOOK! THEY HAVE A BABY!! WE HAVE A BABY, TOO!!

SCENIC POINT

WANT TO SEE PICTURES OF OUR BABY?? MAY I HOLD YOUR BABY?? LUKE, TAKE A PICTURE OF ME HOLDING THE BABY!!!

OH, I MISS OUR BABY!!
I ASSUME THIS IS YOUR FIRST?

OUR FIRST BABY, OR OUR FIRST VACATION AWAY FROM THE BABY?

CATHY SHOULD BE FINISHED GIVING ZENITH HER BATH AND BE CUDDLING UP FOR A LULLABY BEFORE PUTTING HER TO BED RIGHT NOW....

MARK MY WORDS, DEAR. THERE'S NOTHING LIKE CARING FOR SOMEONE ELSE'S SWEET LITTLE BABY TO MAKE A WOMAN'S OWN URGE FOR MOTHERHOOD KICK IN!!
RING, RING

RIP! BONK! SPLASH!
CLANK! MOM! BAM BAM!
SPLOOSH!

HER URGE FOR MOTHER KICKED IN.
IT'S A START...
Guisewite

THE BABY'S RUNNING THROUGH THE HOUSE NAKED, CATHY.
I'VE BEEN TRYING TO GET HER DRESSED AND IN BED FOR THREE HOURS, MOM.

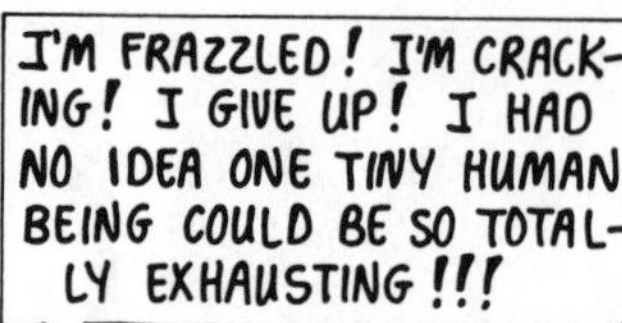
I'M FRAZZLED! I'M CRACKING! I GIVE UP! I HAD NO IDEA ONE TINY HUMAN BEING COULD BE SO TOTALLY EXHAUSTING!!!

WHY AREN'T YOU SAYING ANYTHING?
SOMETIMES IT'S BEST FOR A MOTHER TO KEEP HER MOUTH CLOSED, SWEETIE.

IT KEEPS "I TOLD YOU SO" FROM JUMPING OUT.
Guisewite

LET'S SIT AND WATCH A MOVIE, ZENITH!
WAAAH!

OK. MOVIES ARE OUT. LET'S CALL A FRIEND.
WAAHH!!
FINE. CONVERSATIONS ARE OUT. LET'S DRIVE TO THE STORE.
WAAHH!!

I SEE. ALL ACTIVITIES LASTING MORE THAN THREE SECONDS ARE OUT FOR YOU.

....EXCEPT FOR SMASHING A PAN WITH SPOONS, WHICH YOU CAN DO FOR AN HOUR AND A HALF STRAIGHT.
BAM BAM BAMBAM
BAM BAM BAM BAM BAM BAM BAM BAM BAM BAM BAMBAM BAM BAM BAM
Guisewite

IS MY LITTLE ZENITH EATING HER ASPARAGUS-BASIL SOUP WITH OAT MUFFINS?
SHE'S EATING ANYTHING SHE WANTS, ANDREA.
PARK MAP
PHONE

IS SHE WEARING HER CUTE LITTLE RAW SILK ROMPER WITH MATCHING REEBOKS AND DOING HER NATURAL HISTORY MUSEUM FLASH CARDS?

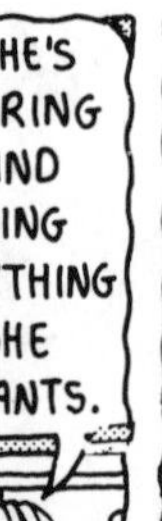
SHE'S WEARING AND DOING ANYTHING SHE WANTS.

IS SHE TAKING HER BOYSENBERRY JUICE BOTTLE TO BED AND SNUGGLING RIGHT TO SLEEP AFTER ONE CD OF DULCIMER MOON SONGS??
SHE SLEEPS WHENEVER, HOWEVER, AND WHEREEVER SHE WANTS.

EVERYTHING'S UNDER AS MUCH CONTROL AS USUAL.
UH-OH.
PARK MAP
PHONE
Guisewite

DON'T GET UP EVERY TIME SHE MAKES A NOISE OR SHE'LL NEVER LEARN TO SLEEP THROUGH THE NIGHT, CATHY.

NEVER LET HER HAVE A SNACK UNTIL SHE'S FINISHED HER DINNER... NEVER LET HER GET AWAY WITH SOMETHING JUST BECAUSE SHE LOOKS CUTE...

PUPPIES ARE LIKE BABIES. THEY NEED A MOTHER WHO GIVES THEM RULES, DISCIPLINE AND CONSISTENTLY FIRM AUTHORITY...
...AND A GRANDMA WHO GIVES THEM ANYTHING THEY WANT!!
Guisewite

ZENITH'S ANIMATED, INTERACTIVE, MICROCHIP-DRIVEN BEAR WITH VOICE, EYE, MOUTH AND PAW MOVEMENTS SYNCHRONIZED TO A SET OF VIDEOTAPE PRODUCTIONS OF "AESOP'S FABLES."

ZENITH'S HANDCRAFTED ITALIAN TEAK BUILDING-BLOCK SET WITH TINY FIGURES OF THE COMPLETE CAST OF THE "CIRQUE DU SOLEIL"... ... ZENITH'S ERGONOMICALLY CORRECT, MONO-FORK, FRONT-SUSPENSION TRICYCLE....

ZENITH'S NATURAL FIBER TYRANNOSAURUS PUPPET THAT SINGS THE FRENCH ALPHABET TO THE TUNE OF "OLD MAC DONALD"... ZENITH'S $300 LIBRARY OF POP-UP BOOKS FROM THE MUSEUM OF MODERN ART....

YOU MAKE ME TOTALLY CRAZY ALL DAY... AND THEN, JUST AFTER I'VE HIT THE CRACKING POINT, YOU DO SOMETHING SO SWEET AND ENDEARING THAT I'D DO ANYTHING IN THE WORLD FOR YOU!

FROM THE TIME WE'RE OLD ENOUGH TO SPEAK, WOMEN VOICE A CERTAIN COMPETITION ABOUT THE MEN IN OUR LIVES.

WITH EVERY YEAR, THE COMPARISONS ARE MORE INTENSE.

UNTIL FINALLY-- CONFIDENT OF OUR TASTES, SURE OF OUR NEEDS--WE REACH THE PINNACLE OF RIVALRY... THAT TRIUMPHANT, SELF-RIGHTEOUS MOMENT THAT MAYBE BEST DEFINES THE STATE OF AFFAIRS BETWEEN MEN AND WOMEN IN THE LATE 1980s....

I THOUGHT YOU WEREN'T SEEING IRVING ANYMORE, CATHY.
I THOUGHT YOU WERE THROUGH WITH FRANKIE, CHARLENE.
LADIES

FRANKIE'S JUST MEETING ME FOR A FRIENDLY DRINK. IT'S NOT A DATE.
IRVING'S JUST STOPPING OVER TO DROP OFF SOME THINGS.

IT'S JUST FRIENDSHIP.
IT'S STRICTLY BUSINESS.
NO BIG DEAL.
A SIMPLE DELIVERY. TOTALLY MEANINGLESS.
SQUIRT
PUFF
DAB
FLUFF
POUF
POUF

DO I LOOK AS RIDICULOUS AS YOU LOOK?
ALMOST. YOU NEED SOME MORE LAVENDER ON THE LIDS.

ANYTHING I CAN DO, CATHY?
NO. I ORDERED DINNER AND DRINKS BY PHONE... MOVIES AND POPCORN ARE BEING DELIVERED LATER... AND I CALLED A MAID TO COME TOMORROW AND CLEAN UP.

FOR ONCE, I WANT A WHOLE, UNINTERRUPTED EVENING TO JUST SIT AND CATCH UP WITH YOU, IRVING!

TO WHOM DO I SPEAK ABOUT HAVING SOME CONVERSATION SENT IN?

CHARLENE?? I THOUGHT YOU WERE OUT WITH FRANKIE.
I'M CALLING FROM THE LADIES ROOM IN THE RESTAURANT, CATHY.
Z Z Z Z

YOU HAVE TO LET FRANKIE AND ME COME OVER. WE'RE DYING HERE! WE NEED TO BE AROUND A FUN, LIVELY COUPLE!!
YOU WANT IRVING AND ME TO SAVE YOUR DATE??

I'M BEGGING YOU, CATHY! WHEN FRANKIE AND I AREN'T SCREAMING AT EACH OTHER ABOUT SOME PAST FIGHT, WE'RE JUST GLARING AT EACH OTHER IN SILENCE... PLEASE!!

WAKE UP, SWEETIE. THE ENTERTAINMENT IS ON THE WAY OVER.
Z Z Z Z

FRANKIE, THIS IS CATHY'S FRIEND IRVING. IRVING IS ONE OF THE FUNNIEST MEN I EVER MET!

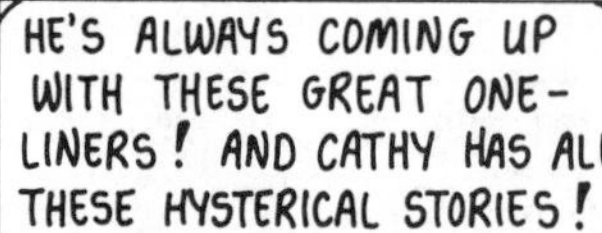
HE'S ALWAYS COMING UP WITH THESE GREAT ONE-LINERS! AND CATHY HAS ALL THESE HYSTERICAL STORIES!

GO AHEAD, YOU TWO! HA, HA! DON'T HOLD BACK!! LET THE WIT ROLL! LET THE HILARITY BEGIN!!

THEY'RE A RIOT, CHARLENE.
I KNEW YOU'D LOVE THEM.
Guisewite

HO, HUM... WE SHOULD BE GOING, CHARLENE.
I'M NOT READY TO GO YET, FRANKIE.

I HAVE TO GET UP EARLY FOR A MEETING. LET'S GO.
WHY DOES YOUR STUPID JOB ALWAYS DICTATE WHEN WE GO??!

MY STUPID JOB PAID FOR YOUR #27 BOWL OF SPAGHETTI!
IT WAS ANGEL HAIR PASTA AND YOU GRABBED THE CHECK!
GRABBED?? YOU WERE IN THE LADIES ROOM FOR 45 MINUTES!!
I ONLY PRIMP BECAUSE YOU'RE SO PICKY!!
HAH!
HAH!

WE'RE STAYING.
I HAVE TO GO.
YOU LIVE HERE, CATHY.
ARE THERE ANY REFRESHMENTS?
Guisewite

DID I TELL YOU ABOUT WHEN FRANKIE...
I AM NOT GOING TO SIT HERE WHILE YOU TELL THAT STUPID STORY FOR THE 400TH TIME, CHARLENE.

HOW DO YOU KNOW WHAT STORY I WAS GOING TO TELL?
I CAN TELL BY HOW YOUR NOSE WRINKLES UP!
I'D RATHER HAVE A NOSE THAT WRINKLES THAN A CHIN THAT WIGGLES!
MY CHIN IS NO WORSE THAN PARTS OF YOU I'M TOO POLITE TO MENTION!

I HATE IT WHEN YOU START AN ARGUMENT AND GET TOO SMUG TO FINISH IT!!
YOU DON'T KNOW HOW TO ARGUE!!
YOU MAKE ME CRAZY!
YOU MAKE ME SICK!!

CHARLENE, WHAT'S GOING ON WITH YOU TWO??
I DON'T KNOW. DO YOU THINK HE LIKES ME??
Guisewite

THE NEXT TIME YOU'RE HAVING A FIGHT WITH YOUR BOYFRIEND, DO **NOT** BRING HIM OVER HERE, CHARLENE.
OH, IT WASN'T THAT BAD, CATHY.

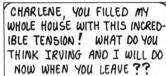

CHARLENE, YOU FILLED MY WHOLE HOUSE WITH THIS INCREDIBLE TENSION! WHAT DO YOU THINK IRVING AND I WILL DO NOW WHEN YOU LEAVE??

INVITE THEM BACK TOMORROW.
GUISEWITE

I'VE SPENT MY WHOLE LIFE OVERCOMING A POOR SELF-IMAGE.

I'VE WORKED, WORKED OUT, DIETED, STUDIED, SWEATED AND STRUGGLED TO DEVELOP A MIND, BODY AND CAREER I COULD FEEL GOOD ABOUT.

NOW--PROUD, ACCOMPLISHED AND TOTALLY SELF-ASSURED-- I WILL CURL UP WITH THE MAN I LOVE AND HEAR THE MOST INCREDIBLE WORDS OF MY LIFE...

YOUR LITTLE INSECURITIES ARE WHAT WILL ALWAYS MAKE YOU SO SPECIAL TO ME, CATHY.
GUISEWITE

WHY HAVEN'T YOU ASKED ABOUT IRVING, MOM?
I THOUGHT I WASN'T SUPPOSED TO ASK ABOUT IRVING ANYMORE.

NO. YOU WEREN'T SUPPOSED TO ASK ABOUT IRVING WHEN I WAS SEEING MITCH... YOU'RE NOT SUPPOSED TO ASK ABOUT **MITCH** ANYMORE... AND YOU'RE **NEVER** SUPPOSED TO ASK ABOUT ANYONE I'VE MENTIONED LESS THAN THREE TIMES OR MORE THAN SIX WEEKS AGO...

... BUT NOW I **WANT** YOU TO ASK ABOUT IRVING! I'VE BEEN **HOPING** YOU'D ASK!!

EVERY TIME I THINK I'M GETTING A GRIP ON THE JOB, SHE REVISES THE TRAINING MANUAL.
GUISEWITE

MY BILLS HAVE ALREADY ALL COME... THE JUNE BRIDES ARE ALL BACK FROM THEIR HONEYMOONS... ALL THE BABIES MY FRIENDS WERE EXPECTING HAVE BEEN BORN AND ANNOUNCED...

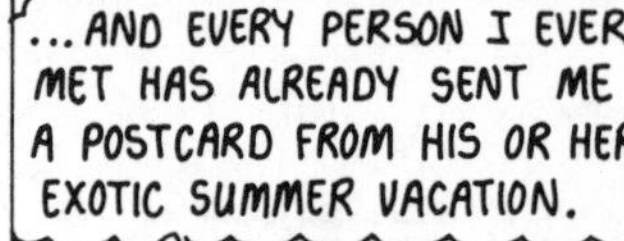
... AND EVERY PERSON I EVER MET HAS ALREADY SENT ME A POSTCARD FROM HIS OR HER EXOTIC SUMMER VACATION.

WE'RE HAVING AN AUGUST WEDDING!!

JUST WHEN I THOUGHT IT WAS SAFE TO GO BACK TO THE MAILBOX....

IF I TAKE IRVING TO THIS WEDDING, HE'LL THINK I'M TRYING TO SNEAK HIM INTO THE "WEDDING SPIRIT," WHICH WOULD BE TRUE.

IF I GO ALONE, PEOPLE WILL THINK I'M LOOKING TO MEET SOMEONE NEW, WHICH WOULD ALSO BE TRUE.

IF I DON'T GO AT ALL, IT WILL LOOK AS IF I'M PARANOID OR JEALOUS OR BOTH, ALL OF WHICH WOULD ALSO BE TRUE.

HOW LARGE OF A GIFT DO I HAVE TO BUY BEFORE I'M ABSOLVED OF ALL SUSPICION?
BRIDAL REGISTRY

MARLA, WHO "WAS NEVER INTO MATERIAL POSSESSIONS," HAS REGISTERED FOR $100-A-DINNER-PLATE CHINA.
COMPUTERIZED BRIDAL REGISTRY

ELAINE, WHO'S EATEN CARRY-OUT CHICKEN WITH A PLASTIC FORK FOR 15 YEARS, IS DOWN FOR $975 STERLING SILVER PLACE SETTINGS.

SHEILA, WHO DRINKS NOTHING BUT DIET COKE, HAS REQUESTED 24 CRYSTAL GOBLETS AT $125 A POP.

CATHY, WHO'S BROKE, IS DUMPING ALL REMAINING WOMEN FRIENDS WHO AREN'T ALREADY MARRIED.
COMPUTERIZED BRIDAL REGISTRY

IRVING...UM, I'M TRYING TO TEACH ELECTRA TO NOT JUMP UP ON THE FURNITURE.
SHE WON'T HURT ANYTHING, CATHY.
COOKIES

I DON'T WANT HER TO BEG FOR FOOD.
IT'S JUST A LITTLE COOKIE.
SHE'S NOT SUPPOSED TO CHEW ON CLOTHING.
HA, HA! LOOK AT HER TUG!

IRVING, IT'S HARD ENOUGH FOR ME TO DISCIPLINE HER WITHOUT YOU HELPING HER BREAK EVERY RULE!
SHE'S JUST HAVING FUN, CATHY! HA, HA!

WHY MOTHERS CONTINUE TO GAIN WEIGHT AFTER THE BABY IS BORN.
COOKIES

WHAT'S YOUR WEDDING GOING TO BE LIKE, SHEILA ?
LOOK! HERE'S MY DRESS! A LONG, BEAUTIFUL WHITE DRESS WITH A 6-FOOT TRAIN!
PROD TEST INC
BRIDE'S

I'M GOING TO HAVE FLOWERS IN MY HAIR AND SATIN SHOES AND EVERYTHING IN THE ROOM IS DESIGNED TO MATCH! FIVE BRIDESMAIDS! FIVE USHERS! BOUQUETS ON EVERY PEW!!
PRODUCT TESTING INC

I'M GOING TO LOOK LIKE A PRINCESS! OH, CATHY, FOR ONE WHOLE DAY I'LL FEEL JUST LIKE A PRINCESS!

I GUESS YOU OPTED FOR TRADITION.
I'M ONLY DOING IT FOR MY MOTHER.

MY FIANCE AND I ASKED OURSELVES, WHICH IS MORE IMPORTANT? A DOWN PAYMENT ON A HOUSE WE'LL OWN FOR 30 YEARS...OR A BEADED VEIL THAT WILL BE ON MY HEAD FOR 45 MINUTES?
BRIDE'S

A BRAND-NEW CAR...OR A SIX-TIER WEDDING CAKE WE'LL TAKE TWO BITES OF? A BASE OF FINANCIAL SECURITY...OR A 4-HOUR $20,000 BASH?? WHAT WOULD YOU HAVE PICKED?
BRIDE'S
THE VEIL, THE CAKE AND THE BASH!
OH, CATHY, IT'LL BE THE HAPPIEST DAY OF OUR LIVES!
BRIDE'S

...THE LAST ONE WE'RE NEVER IN DEBT.
BRIDE'S

WHAT IF MY BRIDESMAIDS DON'T FIT INTO THEIR GOWNS?? WHAT IF THE ORCHIDS DON'T MATCH THE CUMMERBUNDS??

WHAT IF THE CATERER FORGETS THE POACHED SALMON?? WHAT IF THE VIDEO CREW DOESN'T GET ALL THE SHOTS??
SHEILA, RELAX. ONLY ONE THING REALLY MATTERS ON THE BIG DAY.
WHAT IF THEY MISSPELL OUR NAMES ON THE COCKTAIL NAPKINS?!!

ARE YOU NERVOUS ABOUT YOUR WEDDING TOO, PHIL?
WHAT IF SHE STAYS LIKE THIS AFTER WE'RE MARRIED?

WHY DON'T YOU WANT TO GO TO THIS WEDDING WITH ME, IRVING?

BECAUSE WHEN A MAN GOES TO A WEDDING WITH A WOMAN, IT MAKES HER START THINKING ABOUT A WEDDING WITH HIM.
IRVING, GOING TO A WEDDING WITH YOU IS NOT GOING TO MAKE ME START THINKING ABOUT A WEDDING WITH YOU!!

REALLY?
DON'T BE RIDICULOUS.

I HAD OUR WEDDING PLANNED AND OUR CHILDREN'S NAMES PICKED OUT 15 MINUTES AFTER WE MET.

TEN YEARS AGO I WOULD NOT HAVE CHANGED MY NAME IF I GOT MARRIED, BUT NOW IT DOESN'T SEEM SO BAD.... I PLEDGED TO NEVER QUIT MY JOB IF I HAD CHILDREN, BUT NOW I'M SORT OF LOOKING FORWARD TO A SABBATICAL....
YOUR WEDDING

TEN YEARS OF REVOLUTION, AND SUDDENLY I'M WILLINGLY GIVING UP MY NAME, MY CAREER PATH AND EVERY PRIORITY I THOUGHT I HAD.
MODERN BRIDE

SET ONE FOOT IN MY BATHROOM, AND YOU'RE A DEAD MAN, SWEETHEART!!!
YOUR WEDDING

SOME POINTS WILL NEVER BE NEGOTIABLE.
THE SPIRIT LIVES, SHEILA.
YOUR WEDDING

I THOUGHT YOU WERE DEAD SET AGAINST GOING TO THIS WEDDING WITH ME, IRVING.
I WAS... BUT THEN I THOUGHT ABOUT HOW IMPORTANT IT IS TO YOU, CATHY.

REALLY? YOU'RE JUST DOING IT TO MAKE ME HAPPY??
OF COURSE. I'D DO ANYTHING TO MAKE YOU HAPPY.

YOU KNOW WHY I'D DO ANYTHING TO MAKE YOU HAPPY, DON'T YOU, BEAUTIFUL?
YES...

BASEBALL PLAYOFF SEASON IS ONLY A MONTH AWAY.

SHEILA, THE WEDDING WAS JUST BEAUTIFUL. I...
CONGRATULATIONS SHEILA & PHIL

SHE'S **MARRIED! SHE FINALLY GOT MARRIED!** OH, HAPPY DAY!! OH, **THANK THE HEAVENS!!**

OH, KISS THE GROUND! IT'S A **MIRACLE!!** SHE'S **MARRIED!! SHE FINALLY GOT MARRIED!!**

I THINK YOUR MOTHER HAS SUMMED IT UP FOR ALL OF US.
Guisewite

WHAT A WEDDING! THEY MET ONLY 10 MONTHS AGO, BUT THEY JUST KNEW IT WAS RIGHT!
YES. HOW NICE.
CONGRATUL

MY HUSBAND PROPOSED ON OUR THIRD DATE. WE JUST KNEW IT WAS RIGHT, TOO! WHEN IT'S RIGHT, YOU JUST KNOW IT, DON'T YOU THINK?
HA, HA. YES. HOW LOVELY.
CONGRATUL

AND HOW LONG HAVE **YOU TWO** BEEN DATING??
NONE OF YOUR BUSINESS!

MORE THAN FIVE YEARS. I CAN TELL BY HOW HER EYES BUGGED OUT.
STAY AWAY FROM THE PUNCH, MOTHER.
Guisewite

HI. I'M RALPH. UNCLE OF THE BRIDE.... AND YOU MUST BE CATHY AND IRVING, THE **SINGLE PEOPLE! HA, HA!** WHEN ARE YOU TWO TYING THE KNOT??
CONG

HI! MAYBE YOU KIDS WILL BE **NEXT! HA, HA!**
DO WE HEAR **WEDDING BELLS** IN THE FUTURE??
CO

NOTHING LIKE A WEDDING DAY TO POP THE QUESTION!
YOU'D MAKE SUCH A LOVELY BRIDE!
YOU DON'T KNOW HAPPINESS TILL YOU'VE WALKED DOWN THE AISLE!

...SIGH... TO BE SINGLE AGAIN....
CON
Guisewite

I HAD TO CRY AT THE WEDDING BECAUSE IT WAS SO WONDERFUL TO SEE TWO PEOPLE SO MUCH IN LOVE... THEN I CRIED BECAUSE MAYBE I'LL NEVER HAVE THAT....

THEN I CRIED WHEN I MET ALL THE WEIRD RELATIVES BECAUSE I MIGHT TURN INTO ONE. ...THEN I CRIED BECAUSE I WAS SO RELIEVED YOU WERE THERE... THEN I CRIED BECAUSE YOU WERE SEEING ME WITH MASCARA ALL OVER MY FACE...

I DON'T KNOW HOW I'M SUPPOSED TO RESPOND, CATHY.

IF YOU HAVE ANYTHING HORRIBLE TO SAY TO ME, DO IT NOW WHILE I HAVE SOME MOMENTUM.

ONE-STEP MICROWAVE DINNER...
ONE-STEP FURNITURE POLISH...
ONE-STEP FLOOR WAX...
ONE-STEP BATHROOM CLEANER...
ONE-STEP LAUNDRY SOAP...
ONE-STEP OVEN CLEANER...
ONE-STEP VACUUM DEODORIZER...
1 Step FLOOR WAX

FOURTEEN-STEP HAIR CARE SYSTEM.
1 Step FLOOR WAX

1 Step FLOOR WAX

I'M TAKING ALL THE TIME I SAVE MY HANDS AND FEET AND DUMPING IT ON MY HEAD.

BODY POWDER?
LOTION?
OIL?
CREME?
MOUSSE?
GEL?
SPRAY?
TEAL SHADOW?
APRICOT?
TERRA-COTTA?
CHARCOAL?
HAIR UP?
HAIR DOWN?
HAIR BACK?
HAIR CURLED?

SHORT SKIRT?
LONG SKIRT?
MEDIUM SKIRT?
STRAIGHT SKIRT?
FLARED SKIRT?
CAMISOLE?
BLOUSE?
SHORT JACKET?
LONG JACKET?
DRESS?
NUDE HOSE?
OPAQUE HOSE?
SUPPORT HOSE?
NO HOSE?
PANTS?

PUMPS?
FLATS?
OPEN HEEL?
OPEN TOE?
WEDGE?
BELT?
SCARF?
NECKLACE?
BIG EARRINGS?
LITTLE EARRINGS?
PIN?
NAIL POLISH?
HAT?
HUGE PURSE?
TEENSY PURSE?

I WON'T BE IN TO WORK, MR. PINKLEY. I'VE ALREADY USED UP ALL MY DECISION-MAKING SKILLS FOR THE DAY.
Guisewite

IT'S DEPRESSING TO REALIZE WHAT AGE I AM UNTIL I RE-MEMBER WHAT AGE I'LL BE IN JUST A FEW YEARS...

...JUST LIKE IT'S HORRIBLE TO THINK IT'S AUGUST UNTIL I REMEMBER IT WILL BE CHRIST-MAS IN JUST A FEW MONTHS.

IF WE TAKE TIME TO LOOK, LIFE ALWAYS OFFERS A RE-ASSURING PARALLEL FOR US TO CLING TO.

I'M NOT OLD. I'M PRE-HOLIDAY.
Guisewite

5:31.... THE OFFICE IS EMPTY. HOW CAN THE OFFICE BE EMPTY??
IN
IN

LOOK AT ALL THIS WORK! LOOK AT ALL THESE MESSES! LOOK AT ALL THESE EMER-GENCIES!!

WHERE IS EVERYONE?? COME BACK HERE, EVERY-ONE!! COME BACK HERE AND HELP ME DO ALL THIS WORK!!

SOMETIMES I FEEL LIKE A FLY THAT GOT TRAPPED INSIDE AFTER THE PICNIC WAS CARRIED OUT.
Guisewite

TED! WHERE HAVE YOU BEEN?!
I JUST CAME IN TO PACK UP. MY WIFE AND I ARE LEAVING THE STRESS BEHIND AND OPENING A "BED AND BREAKFAST" IN OJAI, CALIF.

BOB AND I ARE LEAVING THE STRESS AND PROVIDING A TOX-IN-FREE ENVIRONMENT FOR OUR CHILDREN BY REINVENTING OUR-SELVES AS FREE-RANGE CHICK-EN FARMERS IN MONTANA!

MY FAMILY AND I ARE SELLING THE CONDO AND MOVING TO A TEPEE IN NEW MEXICO, WHERE WE'LL NOT ONLY PURGE OUR-SELVES OF URBAN STRESS AND TOXINS, BUT EXIST WITH NO CON-TACT WHATSOEVER WITH 1988!

WHAT'S THIS??
THE NEW GENERATION OF OVERACHIEVER QUITTERS.
Guisewite

NO, ELECTRA! BAD GIRL! YOU'RE SUPPOSED TO GO OUTSIDE! BAD BAD BAD!

OH, LOOK AT THAT FACE. DON'T LOOK SO SAD... HERE... HAVE SOME DOG BISCUITS... HAVE A COOKIE... EVERYONE MAKES MISTAKES....

CATHY, YOU'RE SCOLDING HER AND THEN STUFFING HER WITH FOOD TO EASE YOUR CONSCIENCE. I CAN'T BELIEVE MY EYES.

YOU'RE RAISING HER JUST THE WAY I RAISED YOU!!
Guisewite

YOU'RE QUITTING, TED?? JUST LIKE THAT??
EVERYONE'S STARTING TO RETHINK PRIORITIES, CATHY.

WE'VE GIVEN ALL WE HAD TO OUR CAREERS... SACRIFICED EVENINGS, WEEKENDS, RELATIONSHIPS, HEALTH....

I MEAN, AFTER 15 YEARS OF KILLING YOURSELF FOR A JOB, YOU HAVE TO STOP AND ASK YOURSELF SOME PRETTY MAJOR QUESTIONS.

WHERE'S ALL THE MONEY??

EVERYONE USED TO COME BACK FROM VACATION TAN AND READY TO WORK... THIS YEAR, EVERYONE'S COMING BACK PALE AND READY TO QUIT.
IN

WE'RE TIRED OF FEELING BURNED-OUT, CATHY. SICK OF GETTING FRIED. WE'VE LEARNED THE DANGERS OF TOO MUCH HEAT.
IN
SO YOU'RE GIVING UP YOUR WHOLE CAREER??
I'M NOT GIVING UP MY WHOLE CAREER.
FWOMP!
IN

I'M JUST LOOKING FOR A JOB WITH A HIGHER SUN-SCREEN FACTOR.

MR. PINKLEY, I...
OH, THANK HEAVENS IT'S YOU, CATHY! YOU WOULDN'T BELIEVE THE PEOPLE WHO'VE PARADED IN HERE TODAY DEMANDING RAISES!!
PINKLEY
THEY THINK THAT JUST BECAUSE 10 PEOPLE QUIT, THERE ARE 10 SALARIES TO PASS AROUND!!
YOU'RE THE ONE PERSON I KNEW WHO'D HAVE AN ASTUTE ENOUGH GRASP OF THE BIG PICTURE TO NOT TURN OUR CORPORATE CRISIS INTO A QUEST FOR PERSONAL GAIN!!
$5,000 OR I WALK, MR. PINKLEY.

NEXT.

MR. PINKLEY, IN A NORMAL COMPANY, WHEN 10 PEOPLE QUIT, THEY HIRE 10 NEW PEOPLE TO REPLACE THEM.

SOME COMPANIES MIGHT HIRE ONLY **FIVE** NEW PEOPLE, BUT GIVE HUGE RAISES TO THOSE WHO'D BE DOING ALL THE WORK OF THE FIVE THEY DIDN'T REPLACE.

BUT NO COMPANY ON EARTH WOULD LET 10 PEOPLE LEAVE, HIRE NO REPLACEMENTS, AND EXPECT THE MEASLY REMAINING STAFF TO DO ALL THE WORK WITH NO EXTRA MONEY!!

AT LAST! WE'VE FOUND OUR UNIQUE NICHE!!

WHAT A DAY. I'M EXHAUSTED. I CAN'T MOVE.

I WANT SOMEONE TO COME HERE, CLEAN UP MY MESSES, DRESS ME, CARRY ME OUT TO A RESTAURANT AND TELL ME WHAT TO EAT FOR DINNER.

IS IT POSSIBLE TO HIRE A NANNY FOR A HOUSEHOLD IN WHICH THERE ARE NO CHILDREN?

YOU'VE HAD A HARD WEEK. WHY DON'T I BRING SOME DINNER OVER?
THANKS, IRVING, BUT I'M NOT EXACTLY FIXED UP FOR COMPANY...

CATHY, I'VE SEEN YOU "NOT FIXED UP" A HUNDRED TIMES. YOU LOOK GREAT!

I LOVE IT WHEN YOU'RE JUST COMPLETELY NATURAL! I'LL BE RIGHT OVER.
OK... BUT YOU'RE GOING TO SEE THE REAL ME...

...A WOMAN WHO CAN DO A COMPLETE MAKE-OVER IN SIX MINUTES.

HERE, CATHY. NOTHING HELPS GET RID OF STRESS LIKE A MASSAGE.
HE'S FEELING HOW FAT MY SHOULDERS ARE...

TENSIONS EVAPORATE... WORRIES DISAPPEAR...
HE'S SQUASHING THE FAT ON MY BACK... HE'S GOING TO KNEAD THE FAT ON MY WAIST AND THEN ...THEN....

ENOUGH! THANK YOU!! WHEW! THANK YOU! GREAT MASSAGE!!

I HARDLY EVEN STARTED.
THIS IS AS RELAXED AS I CAN STAND TO GET.

THE WHOLE FINKEL CRISIS FELL IN MY LAP TODAY, IRVING!
DID YOU GET IT DONE?

YES. BUT IT WAS CHAOS! A NIGHTMARE!
BUT YOU GOT IT DONE. THAT'S GREAT!

IRVING, IT WAS HORRIBLE! DOWN TO THE WIRE! HEART ATTACK CITY!!
CATHY, YOU MADE IT. YOU'RE HERE. ONLY ONE THING'S IMPORTANT NOW.

FORCING YOU TO LISTEN TO A MINUTE-BY-MINUTE REPLAY.

MOM AND FLO! I THOUGHT YOU TWO WENT OUT OF THE BODY-BUILDING BUSINESS.
OUT?
NO!
CATHY
BODY BY FLO & ANNE

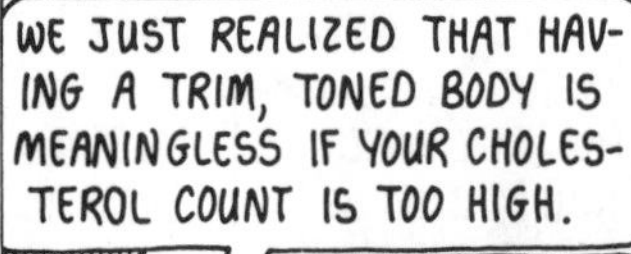
WE JUST REALIZED THAT HAVING A TRIM, TONED BODY IS MEANINGLESS IF YOUR CHOLESTEROL COUNT IS TOO HIGH.

MUFFINS BY FLO & ANNE
BODY BY FLO & ANNE

THUS, FLO WILL CONDUCT A GRUELING WORKOUT, AFTER WHICH I WILL FEED YOU A BIG PLATE OF OAT-BRAN MUFFINS!
A SIMPLE MATTER OF BROADENING OUR CLIENT'S BASES!!
MUFFINS BY FLO & ANNE
BODY BY FLO & ANNE

BROADENING OUR BASE OF CLIENTS.
WHATEVER.
MUFFINS BY FLO & ANNE
BODY BY FLO & ANNE

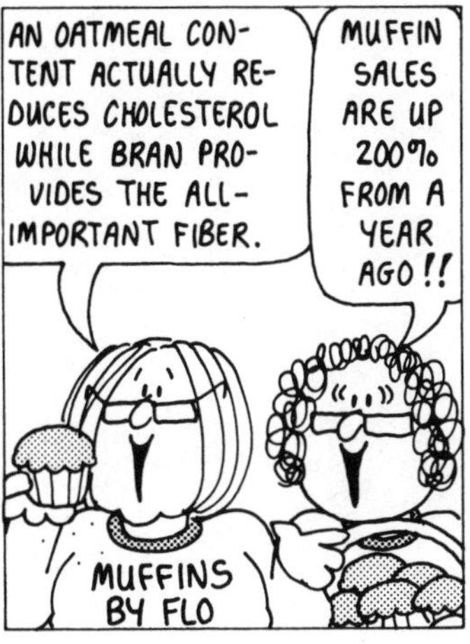

...FOR A TOTAL OF ONLY 36 CALORIES FOR THAT PARTICULAR MUFFIN!

MORE PROOF THAT THE "FAMILY THIGH PROBLEM" BEGINS WITH THE MOUTH.

MUFFINS BY FLO & ANNE

HOW CAN YOU POSSIBLY THINK THIS WILL APPEAL TO THE HECTIC, OVERBOOKED LIFE OF A WORKING PERSON??

IT'S THE MARKETING CONCEPT OF THE '80s, CATHY.

MUFFINS BY FLO & ANNE

BODY BY FLO & ANNE

THE PEOPLE WHO CAN AFFORD THE PROGRAM DON'T HAVE TIME TO ADD UP HOW RIDICULOUS IT IS.

MUFFINS BY FLO & ANNE

BODY BY FLO & ANNE

MOM, YOUR NEW MUFFIN BUSINESS SOUNDS GREAT, BUT I HAVE TO GET BACK TO WORK. I'VE BEEN TRYING TO GET FIVE PEOPLE TOGETHER FOR A MEETING ALL AFTERNOON.
MUFFINS BY FLO & ANNE
BODY BY FLO & ANNE

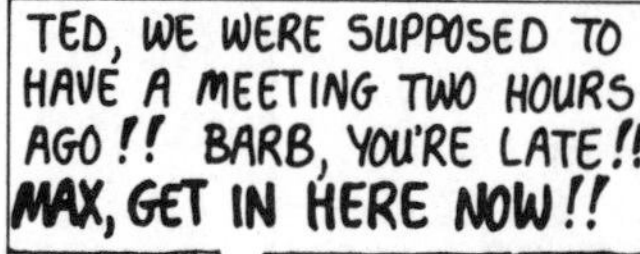
TED, WE WERE SUPPOSED TO HAVE A MEETING TWO HOURS AGO!! BARB, YOU'RE LATE!! MAX, GET IN HERE NOW!!

MUFFINS BY FLO & ANNE
PLOP

NOTHING UNITES US LIKE A GOOD CARBOHYDRATE.
THAT WILL BE $1.29.
GO HOME, MOM.
MUFFINS BY FLO & ANNE
BODY BY FLO & ANNE

IT'S HARD FOR CHILDREN TO HAVE MOTHERS OUT IN THE WORK FORCE INSTEAD OF WAITING AT HOME TO MEET THEIR NEEDS...
MOM, I LIVE IN MY OWN CONDOMINIUM.

EVEN WHEN YOU DON'T LIVE HERE, ON SOME LEVEL YOU EXPECT ME TO BE HERE... AND I JUST WANT TO REASSURE YOU THAT EVEN WHEN I'M NOT HERE, I WILL ALWAYS BE THERE FOR YOU...
MOM, I...

THEREFORE, PLEASE LEAVE A BRIEF MESSAGE AFTER THE BEEP.
AAACK! AN ANSWERING MACHINE!
diet

ALSO, DON'T YELL, SWEETIE. IT STRETCHES YOUR FACE AND MAKES WRINKLES.
diet

SOME WOMEN SHOP EVERY DAY, CONSTANTLY REFINING THEIR OWN TASTES AND NEEDS AS THEY SCRUTINIZE WHAT'S AVAILABLE.
New Arrivals
New Arrivals

SOME WOMEN HAVE A FINE WARDROBE INTACT, AND GO OUT ONCE PER SEASON TO SELECT ACCESSORIES TO UPDATE THEIR ORIGINAL INVESTMENT.

SOME WAIT UNTIL THEY'RE DESPERATE AND THEN FLING THEMSELVES ONTO THE MERCY OF A SALESPERSON WHO WILL TALK THEM INTO TRYING SOMETHING, WHETHER OR NOT IT HAS ANYTHING TO DO WITH THEIR LIVES.

THE BLIND DATE APPROACH TO GETTING DRESSED.
IT'S YOU.

Whine
Yap
Yap
OK, OK. I'LL MOVE YOUR BASKET TO THE BEDROOM, ELECTRA. JUST STOP WHIMPERING.

Whine
Yap
Yap
OK. YOU CAN SLEEP IN MY BED THIS ONCE. JUST BE QUIET.

Yap
Yap
Whine
Whine
FINE. TAKE MY BED. TAKE MY BLANKETS. TAKE MY FOOD. JUST STOP MAKING THAT PATHETIC SOUND! I HAVE TO GET UP IN THREE HOURS!

SLEEP DEPRIVATION: THE FOUNDATION OF ALL GREAT OBEDIENCE PROGRAMS.
Z Z
Z Z Z
Z
COOKIES
Guisewite

THAT'S ADORABLE ON.
NO, THANKS. I'M NOT BUYING UNTIL THE REAL FALL CLOTHES COME OUT THIS YEAR.
NEW
FALL FASHI

THESE **ARE** THE REAL FALL CLOTHES.
NO. THESE ARE THE CLOTHES YOU PUT OUT FOR PEOPLE WHO HIT SEPTEMBER DESPERATE TO SHOP.
NEW

THESE ARE TRANSITIONAL CLOTHES! MADE FOR PEOPLE WITH SO LITTLE IMAGINATION, THEY CAN'T GET FROM LABOR DAY TO HALLOWEEN WITHOUT BUYING CLOTHES THAT ARE APPROPRIATE ONLY FOR TWO WEEKS OF THE YEAR! **HA!**

FOUR ITEMS PER DRESSING ROOM.
DO YOU HAVE ANY TRANSITIONAL SHOES TO GO WITH THESE?
NEW
FALL FASH

THE MOST EXCITING NEWS IN FALL FASHION IS A RETURN TO A MORE CLASSIC FEMININITY!
THAT LOOKS LIKE A MAN'S PIN-STRIPED SUIT.

OH, IT MAY LOOK LIKE A MAN'S SUIT ON THE HANGER, BUT WAIT UNTIL YOU TRY IT ON!

SEE? IN THE RICH TRADITION OF WOMEN'S WEAR, THEY'VE CUT ALL THE PANTS 5 INCHES TOO LONG SO, ONCE AGAIN, YOU'LL HAVE TO START HEMMING EACH AND EVERY THING YOU BUY!!

MOM!
CLASSIC FEMININITY!

THEY CALL IT "DRESSING FOR SAFE SEX."
FALL FASHIONS

THE FASHIONS ARE LONG, SOFTLY PLEATED SKIRTS... FULL, FLOWY JACKETS... AND WIDE PANTS... COVERING EVERY INCH OF THE BODY IN LOOSE, DRAPEY FABRICS...

AFTER A DECADE OF SKIMPY, CLINGY, REVEALING CLOTHES, WOMEN FINALLY HAVE A WHOLE NEW EXPRESSION....

BRING ME A PLATTER OF FETTUCCINE ALFREDO AND A GIANT BASKET OF ROLLS!!!
PASTA

THIS IS FABULOUS! A TIMELESS LOOK THAT WILL BE IN YOUR CLOSET FOR YEARS!
WHAT HAPPENED TO LAST YEAR'S TIMELESS LOOK?
THE NEW TWEEDS

LAST YEAR'S TIMELESS LOOK IS OUT.
YOU SAID IT WOULD BE IN MY CLOSET FOR YEARS.

IS IT STILL IN YOUR CLOSET??
WELL, YES. BUT IT LOOKS RIDICULOUS.

I DIDN'T SAY YOU'D EVER **WEAR** IT, DID I?!
THE NEW TWEEDS

$89 ON NEW CREMES AND MOISTURIZERS TO HELP DIMINISH WRINKLES...
SKIN CARE
Forever Young

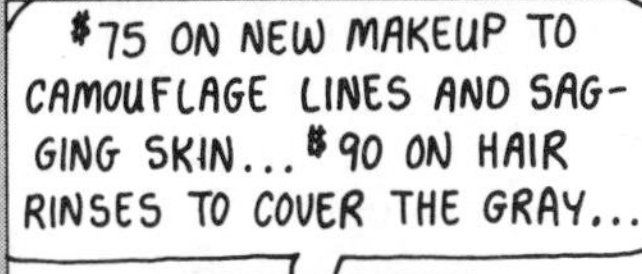
$75 ON NEW MAKEUP TO CAMOUFLAGE LINES AND SAGGING SKIN... $90 ON HAIR RINSES TO COVER THE GRAY...

MAKEUP
Forever Young
$254 ON PRODUCTS WHOSE ONLY PURPOSE IS TO HIDE SIGNS OF AGING.
THIS IS CUTE, CATHY. WHY DON'T YOU TRY IT ON?

IT WOULD MAKE ME LOOK TOO YOUNG.
I GIVE UP.
Forever Young

TA DA! A KICKY NEW LOOK FOR THE WOMAN ON THE GO!
I JUST DON'T THINK A BROWN HERRINGBONE SUIT IS "KICKY."
NEW
NEW

NONSENSE! ADD A DARING CHARTREUSE BLOUSE...DAZZLING PURPLE GLOVES...A RED CHAPEAU...

...THEN WHEN SOMEONE LAUGHS AT YOU AND SAYS YOU LOOK LIKE A MAN, YOU MARCH OVER IN YOUR HOT PINK PUMPS AND **KICK HIM IN THE KNEE!!**

I WANT THE MINISKIRT BACK.

SEE HOW FEMININE THE WIDE PLAID TROUSERS BECOME WITH A TOUCH OF MAGENTA AT THE NECK?

SEE HOW THE 10 YARDS OF FABRIC FLOW OVER YOU, EVER SO SUBTLY OUTLINING YOUR CURVACEOUS, FEMININE LEGS?

SEE HOW THEY SEEM TO SAY, "I'M SO FEMININE, I CAN DRESS LIKE MY UNCLE RALPH AND STILL EXUDE WOMANLY CHARMS"??!

HAH.
SEE WHY FALL '88 IS MAKING MORE AND MORE SALESPEOPLE START LOOKING FOR NEW CAREERS?
Guisewite

THE NEW BOLERO JACKET... THE NEW TROUSERS... ALL YOU NEED ARE SOME BLACK SUEDE PUMPS.
I'M WEARING BLACK SUEDE PUMPS.
NEW

AH, BUT YOUR BLACK SUEDE PUMPS HAVE THE OLD HEEL. SEE? THE 1988 HEEL CURVES IN EVER SO SLIGHTLY AT THE TIP... A SENSUOUS CONTOUR THAT CHANGES THE WHOLE MOOD OF THE OUTFIT TO ONE OF PROVOCATIVE FLIRTATION.

MY BOYFRIEND HAS NEVER EVEN LOOKED AT THE FRONTS OF THE SHOES I ALREADY OWN. HE IS NOT GOING TO RESPOND TO A 1/8" CURVE ON THE TIP OF A HEEL!!!

YOU'LL KNOW IT'S THERE.
THE SHOE DEPARTMENT IS NEXT TO FRAGRANCES, WHERE YOU'LL ALSO WANT TO STOP. YOUR COLOGNE REEKS OF 1987.

WOMEN WANTED TO BE SEXIER.. ...THEN REJECTED THE MINISKIRT AS TOO "TRAMPY." YOU WANTED TO BE MORE PROFESSIONAL... THEN REJECTED THE BUSINESS SUIT AS TOO "STUFFY."
NEW SHORT
NEW MEDIUM
NEW LONG

YOU WANTED TO BE MORE FEMININE... THEN REJECTED THE BUBBLE DRESS AS TOO "CUTESY." FINE. WE GIVE UP.

EVERY CONCEIVABLE SHAPE, SIZE AND LENGTH IS HERE THIS YEAR. YOU'RE ON YOUR OWN! WE'RE SICK OF HEARING WHAT WOMEN WANT ONLY TO HAVE YOU POOH-POOH IT AFTER WE KILL OURSELVES TRYING TO PROVIDE IT!
NEW WIDE
NEW LONG

YES! BRAVO! WELL PUT!!
NOW, MORE THAN EVER, LEAVE YOUR MALE FRIENDS AT HOME WHEN YOU GO SHOPPING.
NEW LONG
CLAP CLAP CLAP CLAP
Guisewite

NEVER WEAR TWO-TONE OUTFITS. YOU'LL LOOK CHOPPY AND SHORT.
TRY THIS TURQUOISE BLOUSE OVER THIS PURPLE SKIRT!

NEVER WEAR PATTERNS. YOU'LL LOOK BULKY.
PUT A GLEN PLAID JACKET OVER IT...
NEVER WEAR TRENDY ACCESSORIES. YOU'LL LOOK CHEAP.
...AND A JUMBO FAUX-CROCODILE BELT!

YOU'RE RIGHT, MOM. I LOOK CHOPPY, SHORT, BULKY AND CHEAP.
NO! YOU LOOK BEAUTIFUL! OH, DOESN'T SHE LOOK JUST BEAUTIFUL!!

MOTHERLY ADVICE AND MOTHERLY SUPPORT CLASH HEAD-ON IN DRESSING ROOM #5.
GUISEWITE

REMEMBER, CATHY. FOR EACH NEW ITEM OF CLOTHING BOUGHT, AN OLD ITEM MUST BE REMOVED FROM THE CLOSET!
RIGHT, MOM. HEE, HEE...

HEE, HEE...NOTHING GETS HUNG UNTIL IT'S PERFECTLY ALTERED AND PRESSED!
HEE HEE HEE

HA, HA!... AN HOUR SPENT ORGANIZING AT THE BEGINNING OF THE SEASON WILL SAVE HUNDREDS OF HOURS LATER ON! HA, HA! HOO HA HA!
HA HA!
HOO HA!

WHY IS IT WE HAVE SOME OF OUR BEST TIMES TOGETHER WHEN WE'RE RIDICULING MY RULES FOR LIVING?
GUISEWITE

WE'VE WATCHED THE CANDIDATES IN ACTION... SEEN THEIR VIDEOS.. ..HEARD THEIR SOUND BITES... READ THEIR CLAIMS... ARGUED WITH OUR FRIENDS...

AND NOW, IN THE RICHEST TRADITION OF AMERICA, WE NEED EACH TO SIT ALONE, GATHER THE INFORMATION AROUND US...

...AND EVER SO CALMLY AND QUIETLY BEGIN TO ASK OURSELVES THE QUESTION WE ASK AT LEAST ONCE EVERY FOUR YEARS....

IS THERE STILL HOPE FOR LIFE ON MARS?

IF ELECTED, I WILL APPOINT A SPECIAL TASK FORCE TO STUDY NEW TECHNIQUES FOR BALANCING THE BUDGET...
OH, FOR HEAVEN'S SAKE. JUST QUIT SPENDING MONEY YOU DON'T HAVE!

I WILL COMMISSION ADVISORY REPORTS ON WHAT TO DO ABOUT OUR ICKY OCEANS AND RIVERS...
IF YOU MESS IT UP, YOU CLEAN IT UP! WHAT'S SO HARD ABOUT THAT?

I WILL CONTINUE TO INVEST IN A STRONG DEFENSE TO KEEP THIS COUNTRY A SAFE PLACE FOR THE HOMELESS PEOPLE TO LIVE!
SEND YOURSELF TO BED WITH NO DINNER, YOUNG MAN!!!

THIS COUNTRY DOESN'T NEED A PRESIDENT. IT NEEDS A MOTHER.

SENATE REPUBLICANS KILLED A DAY CARE SUBSIDY PLAN THIS MONTH, PREFERRING TO BACK BUSH'S PLAN TO GIVE FAMILIES A $1,000 TAX CREDIT FOR EACH CHILD UNDER AGE 4.

THE BUSH PLAN COMES TO $2.74 PER DAY PER CHILD. WHILE NO ONE COULD FIND DECENT DAY CARE FOR $2.74 A DAY, HIS PLAN WOULD ALLOW EACH IMPOVERISHED FAMILY TO BUY A DECENT VCR.

NOT ONLY WOULD CHILDREN HAVE SOMETHING TO WATCH WHILE MOMMY RIPS HER HAIR OUT, BUT EACH VCR PURCHASE WOULD FURTHER BOOST THE JAPANESE ECONOMY SO THEY COULD KEEP BOOSTING OUR ECONOMY BY BUYING UP ALL OUR BUILDINGS AND BUSINESSES.

PARENTS, OF COURSE, COULD TAPE ALL SPEECHES EXPLAINING HOW WELL OFF WE ARE.
GET YOUR BOTTLE, HONEY. MOMMY HAS TO GO TO BED FOR FOUR YEARS.

I LOST MY JOB WHEN I HAD A BABY BECAUSE REPUBLICANS BELIEVE MATERNITY LEAVES SHOULD BE DECIDED ON BY INDIVIDUAL COMPANIES, AND MY COMPANY DECIDED NOT TO GIVE THEM.

I CAN'T AFFORD TO GET ANOTHER JOB BECAUSE REPUBLICANS BELIEVE DAY CARE HELP SHOULD BE THE CHOICE OF INDIVIDUAL COMPANIES, AND THE 10,000 COMPANIES I'VE APPLIED TO HAVE CHOSEN NOT TO OFFER IT.

THIS WOULD ALL MAKE ME SICK EXCEPT REPUBLICANS BELIEVE HEALTH CARE SHOULD BE A PERSONAL MATTER, AND I AM A PERSON WHO'S UNEMPLOYED, UNINSURED AND INELIGIBLE FOR AID.

IT WAS EASIER TO SUPPORT THE CONCEPT OF GIVING POWER TO THE INDIVIDUAL WHEN I WAS AN INDIVIDUAL WHO HAD SOME.

TALKING ABOUT WHAT I WANT IN A RELATIONSHIP IS TORTURE FOR ME, CATHY.
YOU'RE SO DAR-LING...

OH. REALLY? WELL, I MEAN, I CAN DO IT... I JUST.....
YOU'RE SO SMART. YOU'RE SO BRAVE. I LOVE YOU!!

IT'S NOT SO BAD! LET'S TALK! LET'S TALK ABOUT WHAT WE WANT!
YOU'RE SO PRECIOUS, ELECTRA! HERE'S A NICE, BIG SNACK!

I WANT TO BE REINCAR-NATED AS A DOG.

THE REAGAN-BUSH ADMINISTRATION HAS DONE NOTHING ABOUT THE FACT THAT 44% OF THE WORK FORCE IS WOMEN, BUT WE STILL HAVE NO NATIONAL LAW REQUIRING EQUAL PAY.

IT'S DONE NOTHING ABOUT THE FACT THAT 67% OF THE WOMEN WHO HAVE PRESCHOOL CHILDREN WORK FULL TIME AND NEED DAY CARE HELP... NOTHING ABOUT THE FACT THAT ALMOST 90% OF THE FAMILIES ON WELFARE ARE SINGLE MOTHERS WITH NO WAY OUT.

YET, INCREDIBLY, MANY PEOPLE LOOK AT THE CURRENT GOVERNMENT AND THINK THINGS ARE GOING PRETTY WELL.

THE GOVERNMENT IS LIKE A BABY. IT LOOKS LIKE A LITTLE ANGEL WHEN IT'S SLEEPING.
Guisewite

BY NOV. 8, $65 MILLION WILL HAVE BEEN SPENT IN THE PRESIDENTIAL RACE. BECAUSE OF THE GOVERNMENT'S FUND-MATCHING PROGRAM, APPROXIMATELY ONE-FOURTH OF THAT WILL HAVE BEEN FROM OUR OWN INCOME TAX DOLLARS.

CANDIDATES WILL HAVE SPENT $16 MILLION OF OUR OWN HARD-EARNED MONEY TRYING TO CONVINCE US THEY'RE MOST QUALIFIED TO MANAGE THE FINANCES OF THE COUNTRY...

WHILE THE RESULT IS STILL SPECULATION, THERE'S A GROWING FEELING THAT WE'LL BE HEARING ONE STRONG, UNIFIED VOICE ON ELECTION DAY...

I WANT A REFUND!!!
Guisewite

HI, ZENITH! AREN'T YOU CUTE?!
I CONVINCED HER THE ONLY MEANINGFUL COSTUME FOR AN ELECTION YEAR WAS THE STATUE OF LIBERTY.
Trick or Treat

SEE? WHEN PEOPLE GIVE HER CANDY, SHE HANDS THEM A FLIER EXPLAINING HOW IMPORTANT IT IS FOR EACH AND EVERY PERSON TO VOTE!

NOT ONLY IS ZENITH REMINDING PEOPLE ABOUT ONE OF OUR MOST PRECIOUS RIGHTS, BUT SHE'S LEARNING A VALUABLE LESSON ABOUT WHAT'S IN STORE FOR HER OWN FUTURE!!

THERAPY BY AGE 5.
Guisewite

WHAT'S ALL THIS, ANDREA ?
THIS YEAR THE WOMEN'S VOTE IS MORE CRITICAL THAN EVER, CATHY.

NOT ONLY ARE WE ELECTING A PRESIDENT, BUT THE NEXT PRESIDENT WILL PROBABLY APPOINT AT LEAST THREE SUPREME COURT JUSTICES WHOSE POSITIONS ON WOMEN'S ISSUES COULD SHAPE THE FUTURE FOR OUR CHILDREN FOR ANOTHER 30 YEARS.

BY HAVING ZENITH'S PLAY GROUP JOIN ME IN CANVASSING THE NEIGHBORHOOD, WE'RE TURNING A GRASS ROOTS CAMPAIGN INTO SOMETHING MUCH, MUCH MORE!

A GRASS STAIN CAMPAIGN.

LOOK WHAT MOMMY WROTE, ZENITH... "25% OF THE CHILDREN IN THE COUNTRY TODAY LIVE WITH A SINGLE PARENT. WE NEED DUKAKIS BECAUSE HE SUPPORTS A NATIONAL DAY-CARE PLAN AND LAWS TO RAISE DAY-CARE STANDARDS."
COPY SHOP

"44% OF THE WORKFORCE ARE WOMEN, BUT WOMEN EARN ONLY 64% OF WHAT MEN DO. WE NEED DUKAKIS BECAUSE HE SUPPORTS LAWS FOR EQUAL PAY."
COPY SHOP

"80% OF THE WOMEN WILL GET PREGNANT DURING THEIR WORKING LIVES. WE NEED DUKAKIS BECAUSE HE SUPPORTS JOB-PROTECTED MATERNITY LEAVES."
SPLOOSH!
COPY SHOP

...AND 99% OF ALL CHILDREN UNDER AGE 3 WILL STUFF POLITICAL FLIERS DOWN THE TOILET BEFORE MOMMY HAS A CHANCE TO HAND THEM OUT.

SINCE 1981, AID TO EDUCATION HAS BEEN CUT BY 16%... FUNDS FOR WATER POLLUTION CONTROL HAVE BEEN CUT BY 43%... CHILD-CARE FUNDING HAS BEEN CUT BY 28%... THE MINIMUM WAGE HAS DROPPED IN REAL VALUE BY 31%...

ANDREA, THERE'S NOTHING AS ANNOYING AS SOMEONE WHO'S STOPPED BY THE DEMOCRATIC HEADQUARTERS AND PICKED UP A BUNCH OF THEIR STATISTICS.

IF YOU WANT TO TALK POLITICS, COME BACK WHEN YOU HAVE FAIR, NON-PARTISAN, NON-SUBJECTIVE FACTS.
DING DONG!

FOUR OUT OF THE LAST 10 VICE PRESIDENTS BECAME PRESIDENT.

WHEN REPUBLICANS TALK ABOUT THE THRIVING ECONOMY THEY'VE BUILT, THEY DON'T MENTION THAT THEIR ECONOMY REQUIRES MOST MOTHERS TO WORK OUTSIDE THE HOME TO TRY TO HELP PAY THE BILLS.

WHEN THEY TALK ABOUT FAMILY VALUES, THEY DON'T MENTION THAT THEY'VE CONSISTENTLY VOTED AGAINST ANY LEGISLATION THAT WOULD HELP STRUGGLING WORKING MOTHERS OUT OF THE HOLE.

WHEN WOMEN HAVE NO CHOICE BUT TO WORK MORE AND SPEND LESS TIME WITH THEIR CHILDREN, WHAT DO REPUBLICANS THINK ALL THOSE CHILDREN ARE GOING TO DO?!
CHILDREN WILL DO WHAT THEY'VE ALWAYS DONE, ANDREA.

GROW UP AND BLAME THEIR MOTHERS.

IN A STARTLING ELECTION POLL REVERSAL, 93% OF ALL AMERICAN VOTERS NOW REPORT BEING MIFFED THAT NO ONE EVER CALLS THEM WHEN THEY'RE CONDUCTING POLLS.

THIS IS UP FROM LAST WEEK'S POLL, WHICH SHOWED THAT 52% WOULD RATHER LISTEN TO POLLS THAN WATCH THE NEW FALL TV SEASON.

WHILE 37% THINK THE POLLS **ARE** THE NEW FALL TV SEASON, THE 76% WHO FORMERLY SAID THEY IGNORE POLLS ARE NOW DIVIDED AMONG 8% WHO LIKE POLLS, 27% WHO MAKE UP THEIR OWN POLLS, AND 41% WHO SAY THEY'LL VOTE AGAINST POLLS JUST TO PUT THEM OUT OF BUSINESS.

AND NOW LET'S HEAR WHAT THE CANDIDATES ARE SAYING IN THESE CRITICAL LAST DAYS BEFORE THE ELECTION...
OOPS. SORRY. WE'RE OUT OF TIME, JOHN...
CLICK!

"A 'YES' VOTE ON THIS PROPOSITION MEANS YES, YOU ARE NOT FOR IT."
OFFICIAL SAMPLE BALLOT

"A 'YES' ON THIS PROPOSITION MEANS YES, YOU WANT THEM TO CEASE SPENDING MONEY TO OPPOSE ITS OBJECTORS."
OFFICIAL SAMPLE BALLOT

"A 'YES' ON THIS PROPOSITION MEANS YES, YOU DO NOT WANT THEM TO QUIT THE CANCELLATION OF LOOSER RESTRICTIONS PREVIOUSLY VOTED DOWN BY PROPONENTS OF THIS MEASURE."
OFFICIAL SAMPLE BALLOT

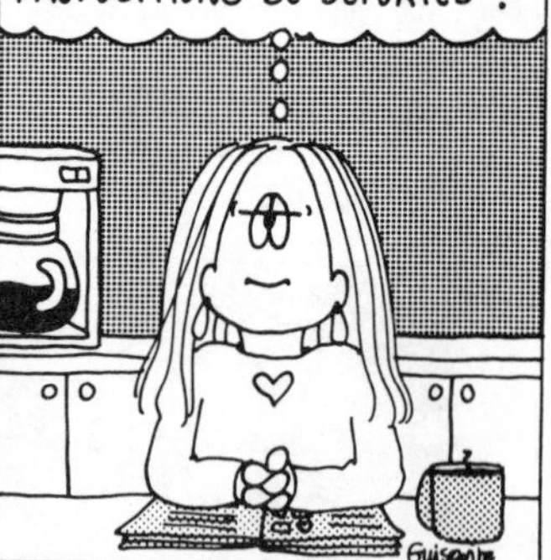
WHERE'S THE PROPOSITION SUGGESTING THAT THE PEOPLE RESPONSIBLE FOR WORDING THE PROPOSITIONS BE DEPORTED?

IN THE GREAT AMERICAN TRADITION OF INDEPENDENCE, WE EACH HAVE OUR OWN IDEAS ABOUT WHAT'S BEST FOR THE COUNTRY.
VOTE

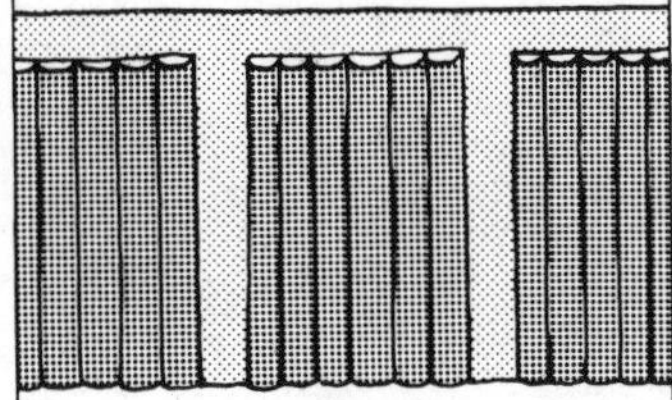
IN THE GREAT AMERICAN TRADITION OF DEMOCRACY, WE CAST OUR VOTES FOR THE PEOPLE WE FIRMLY BELIEVE WILL ENSURE A PROSPEROUS, PEACEFUL, PRODUCTIVE, HAPPY FUTURE FOR OURSELVES AND OUR LOVED ONES.

VOTE

IN THE GREAT AMERICAN TRADITION OF HEDGING OUR BETS, WE STOP ON THE WAY HOME AND BUY A LOTTERY TICKET.
LOTTERY TICKETS
SLURPEE

MY HIGH-POWERED, STEEL-BLUE GABARDINE SUIT WITH NO-NONSENSE SILK CREPE BLOUSE... NOT HERE.

MY SOPHISTICATED KNIT DRESS, WHICH EXUDES CONFIDENCE AND CONTROL... NOT HERE.

MY ELEGANTLY FEMININE BLAZER AND FLARED SKIRT, FOR AN AIR OF WARM, YET REGAL, AUTHORITY... NOT HERE.

I HAVE A LOT OF POTENTIAL, BUT IT'S ALL AT THE DRY CLEANERS.
RECEPTIONIST
Go Team

HI, IRVING... WHAT ARE YOU DOING??
WHAT DO YOU MEAN, WHAT AM I DOING?

I THOUGHT, YOU KNOW... YOU MIGHT LIKE SOME COMPANY...
IT'S THE MIDDLE OF THE DAY.
I KNOW... HEH, HEH... A LITTLE EARLY SNUGGLE?...

SNUGGLE?? CATHY, TODAY IS THE MICHIGAN-OHIO STATE GAME!! ARE YOU KIDDING? ARE YOU OUT OF YOUR MIND??!!

THE PEOPLE WHO PUBLISH SEDUCTION ARTICLES SHOULD PRINT FOOTBALL SCHEDULES.

...AND THIS BY THE END OF THE YEAR ?! HA, HA! THAT'S A GOOD ONE! HAVE YOU EVER SEEN THIS PLACE BETWEEN THANKSGIVING AND THE END OF THE YEAR?!! HA, HA, HOO HA HA!!

ELECTRA, MY PUPPY, IS WAITING FOR ME AT HOME. WHAT A WONDERFUL FEELING!

SHE'S THERE...WAITING JUST FOR ME! FOR THE FIRST TIME IN MY LIFE, I FINALLY UNDERSTAND WHAT MY FRIENDS HAVE BEEN SAYING ABOUT THEIR CHILDREN ALL THESE YEARS....

AACK!
ARF!

THEY ALWAYS NEED A HUG JUST WHEN YOU NEED TO SCREAM AT THEM.

HOW'S THANKS-GIVING DINNER COMING?
WONDERFUL! I LET CATHY STEW OVER MY CRITIQUE OF HER HAIR WHILE I GRILLED HER ABOUT HER FUTURE WITH IRVING!
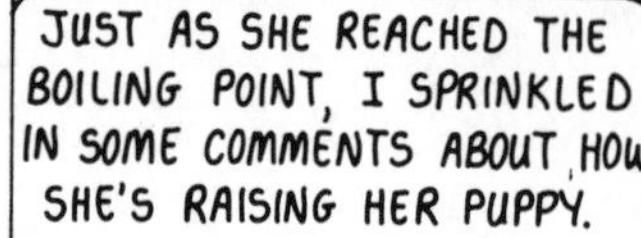
JUST AS SHE REACHED THE BOILING POINT, I SPRINKLED IN SOME COMMENTS ABOUT HOW SHE'S RAISING HER PUPPY.

I'M LETTING THAT SIMMER FOR ABOUT 20 MINUTES... ..THEN I'LL CHOP UP HER DE-FENSE OF HER CAREER PATH... ...TOSS IN SOME FREE ADVICE ABOUT HER WARDROBE... AND LET THE WHOLE WORKS FRY!!

IS ANY ACTUAL FOOD BEING PRE-PARED IN HERE?
WHO HAS TIME FOR FOOD?

WHERE'S THE REST OF THE PIE, CATHY?
MOM HID IT SO I WOULDN'T EAT IT, DAD.

WHAT IF I WANT SOME?
SHE HID IT SO YOU WOULDN'T EAT IT, EITHER.

AFTER ALL OUR SPEECHES YES-TERDAY ABOUT HOW WE WERE NEVER TOUCHING ANOTHER PIECE OF PIE, MOM SAID IT WAS HER DUTY TO PUT THE PIE WHERE NEITHER OF US COULD GET TO IT.

THE SACRIFICES I MAKE FOR MY FAMILY....

ARE YOU SURE YOU CAN'T STAY FOR DINNER, CATHY?
MOM, ALL WE'VE DONE FOR TWO DAYS IS EAT.

WE GET UP AND EAT... GO OUT AND EAT... COME HOME AND EAT.... I HAVE 10 MIL-LION THINGS TO DO THIS WEEK-END. I AM NOT GOING TO SPEND ANY MORE TIME EATING!

HI, IRVING. WANT TO GO GET SOMETHING TO EAT?

CHARLENE, WITH FOUR SHORT WEEKS UNTIL CHRISTMAS, IT'S TIME TO DELIVER THE ANNUAL PRE-HOLIDAY MESSAGE.
CERTAINLY, MR. PINKLEY.

ATTENTION ALL EMPLOYEES: THIS MARKS THE LAST WEEK FOR SINGLE PEOPLE TO MEET SOMEONE AND HAVE ANY HOPE OF SHARING THE ROMANCE OF THE HOLIDAYS WITH ANYONE BESIDES OUR HOUSE PETS.

IF YOU HAVE A GRAIN OF COMPASSION IN YOUR PORES, YOU WILL THINK OF SOMEONE TO FIX ME UP WITH AND **YOU WILL DO IT TODAY**!!!

I MEANT THE MESSAGE ABOUT NOT SLACKING OFF ON OUR WORK LOADS.
GET YOUR OWN MICROPHONE.

WHATEVER HAPPENED TO STAN, CHARLENE?
WE'RE FRIENDS, BUT THERE WILL NEVER BE ANY REAL ATTACHMENT. WHAT ABOUT MITCH?

WE'RE IN TOUCH, BUT NOTHING SERIOUS. WHAT ABOUT JOHN?
A LUNCH HERE, A DRINK THERE. NO BIG DEAL.

WE HAVE ALL THESE LITTLE PIECES OF RELATIONSHIPS STUCK TO OUR LIVES, BUT NOTHING THAT'S EVER REALLY GOING TO LAST, CATHY.
YEAH... I KNOW WHAT YOU MEAN...

WE'RE IN THE "POST-IT NOTE" YEARS OF OUR DATING LIVES.

ANXIOUS TO LOOK ATTRACTIVE AND AVAILABLE, I PLASTER THE MAKEUP ON...
TOWELS

EMBARRASSED THAT I LOOK AS IF I'M **TRYING** TO LOOK AVAILABLE, I WIPE THE MAKEUP OFF.
TOWELS

ANNOYED THAT I SPENT $50 ON MAKEUP I'M EMBARRASSED TO WEAR, I PLASTER THE MAKEUP BACK ON... FURIOUS THAT I LET A SALESCLERK TALK ME INTO A LOOK I DON'T LIKE, I WIPE THE MAKEUP BACK OFF.....

THE QUESTION IS NOT WHY THERE'S ALWAYS A LINE TO GET INTO THE LADIES' ROOM... THE QUESTION IS HOW A WOMAN EVER GETS OUT OF ONE.

MAY I COME IN THE KITCHEN YET, CATHY?
NO, YOU MAY NOT COME IN YET!

WHAT ARE YOU DOING IN THERE?
IRVING, I HAVE CATALOGS TO GO THROUGH...GIFTS TO FIGURE OUT... CARDS TO ADDRESS ...LISTS TO MAKE...

CHRISTMAS IS LESS THAN FOUR WEEKS AWAY! I'M DOING WHAT EVERY WOMAN IN THE COUNTRY IS DOING TONIGHT!!!

HOW OPRAH LOST THE WEIGHT

FRANKIE DOESN'T CALL BECAUSE HE'S AFRAID I'LL GET HURT... I WON'T CALL ANYONE BEFORE I'M RECOVERED FROM FRANKIE BECAUSE I'M AFRAID THE NEW PERSON WOULD GET HURT...

EVEN IF I **WERE** RECOVERED FROM FRANKIE, I WOULDN'T CALL ANYONE NEW BECAUSE I MIGHT CHANGE MY MIND AND HE'D GET HURT...IF FRANKIE THOUGHT I WAS EVEN **THINKING** OF SOMEONE NEW, HE'D GET HURT...

IF I **DON'T** TRY TO MEET ANYONE, I **MIGHT** GET HURT...BUT IF I **GET** HURT, I WILL **DEFINITELY** GO MEET SOMEONE AND THEN **HE** WOULD GET HURT, **I** WOULD GET HURT AND **FRANKIE** WOULD GET HURT.

NO ONE ACTUALLY DATES ANYMORE, CHARLENE. WE'RE ALL JUST PROTECTING EACH OTHER.

PEOPLE WHO MOVED, BUT I CAN'T FIND THEIR NEW ADDRESSES... PEOPLE WHO HAVE THE SAME ADDRESS, BUT I NEVER WROTE DOWN THEIR ZIP CODE...
CARDS TO DO

PEOPLE WHO GOT MARRIED, BUT I CAN'T REMEMBER WHAT NAME THEY USE...PEOPLE WHO SPLIT UP, BUT I DON'T KNOW WHO STAYED IN THE HOUSE, WHO MOVED OUT, OR WHERE THE PERSON WHO MOVED WENT...
CARDS TO DO
CARDS TO DO

PEOPLE WHOSE CHILDREN SHOULD BE INCLUDED ON THE ADDRESS, BUT I DON'T REMEMBER THEIR NAMES, THEIR SEXES, OR HOW MANY OF THEM THERE ARE.

I'VE GIVEN UP THE NOTION OF WRITING LONG, PERSONAL NOTES, AND AM STRIVING ONLY TO COMPLETE ONE ENVELOPE.
CARDS TO DO
CARDS TO DO

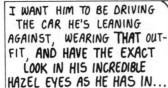

HELLO. I'D LIKE THE MAN ON PAGE 23 SENT TO MY HOME IMMEDIATELY.
Holiday GIFTS

I WANT HIM TO BE DRIVING THE CAR HE'S LEANING AGAINST, WEARING THAT OUTFIT, AND HAVE THE EXACT LOOK IN HIS INCREDIBLE HAZEL EYES AS HE HAS IN...
Holiday

.... I BEG YOUR PARDON? OH. YES... I SEE. WELL, THANK YOU ANYWAY.
Holiday GIFTS

HOW'S THE CATALOG SHOPPING COMING, CATHY?
I'M NOT GETTING ANY MORE GIFTS, BUT I'M HAVING A BETTER TIME LOOKING.

"OH, DARLING," HE'LL SAY, "I'LL CARRY IT ALWAYS AND THINK OF YOU".... HE'LL CARRY IT ON HIS NEXT BUSINESS TRIP AND THINK OF ME.....
FINE ITALIAN ATTACHÉS

THE WOMAN NEXT TO HIM ON THE PLANE WILL BE IMPRESSED BY ITS INCREDIBLE STYLE... THEY'LL CHAT AND LAUGH...HE'LL START POSTPONING HIS TRIP HOME... HIS CALLS WILL STOP... THE OPERATOR WON'T LET ME THROUGH TO HIS ROOM ANYMORE...

AAACK!!
CATHY! WHAT HAPPENED??

SOMEWHERE BETWEEN THE DISPLAY AREA AND THE CASHIER, MY ROMANTIC FANTASY QUIT HAVING ME IN IT.

THIS SWEATER IS PERFECT!
IRVING WOULDN'T WEAR A SWEATER LIKE THAT.
FOR HIM
BUT HE'D LOOK SO GREAT IN IT!
CATHY, NEVER GIVE A MAN SOMETHING THAT MATCHES YOUR TASTE INSTEAD OF HIS!
FOR HIM

IT SAYS YOU'RE TRYING TO TRANSFORM HIM... YOU'RE CRITICAL OF HIS USUAL STYLE... INSENSITIVE TO HOW UNCOMFORTABLE HE'D BE ABOUT HAVING TO WEAR SOMETHING YOU GAVE HIM... AND TOTALLY OBLIVIOUS TO HIS OWN SENSE OF HIMSELF!

THAT WILL BE $88.95.
THEN AGAIN, HOW OFTEN DO YOU COME ACROSS A GIFT WITH THIS MUCH MEANING?
FOR HIM

WHY CAN'T YOU STAY WITH US THROUGH NEW YEAR'S WHEN YOU COME FOR CHRISTMAS, SWEETIE?
MOM, WE'VE HAD THIS DISCUSSION EVERY YEAR OF MY LIFE SINCE I LEFT HOME.

IT COMES OUT EXACTLY THE SAME EVERY TIME.

CAN'T WE JUST SKIP THE BEGINNING AND MIDDLE AND GO RIGHT TO THE CONCLUSION?
DON'T BE RIDICULOUS.

DURING HOLIDAYS IT'S IMPORTANT TO DO EVERYTHING FROM SCRATCH.
Guisewite

CHRISTMAS ISN'T FOR TWO WEEKS! WHAT'S WRONG WITH YOU PEOPLE?? GO HOME! GET OUT OF MY PARKING SPOTS!

I HAVE TO BUY A PAIR OF SHOES TO WEAR TONIGHT! I ONLY HAVE AN HOUR AND A HALF TO SHOP! YOU HAVE TWO WEEKS!!

CLEAR THE WAY! LET ME THROUGH!! I'M NOT HERE TO BUY GIFTS! I'M SHOPPING FOR ME! I'M JUST TRYING TO BUY THINGS FOR ME!!!

IF STORES REALLY UNDERSTOOD THE HOLIDAY SPIRIT, THEY'D OPEN AN EXPRESS LANE FOR THE GREEDY.
Guisewite

"DURING THE FRANTIC HOLIDAY SEASON, IT'S IMPORTANT TO TAKE TIME TO PAMPER YOUR OVEREXERTED SENSES..."
HOLIDAY TIPS

"INVEST IN A SOOTHING, HOUR-LONG PROFESSIONAL MASSAGE... THEN HAVE A LONG, LUXURIOUS BUBBLE BATH, TAKING TIME TO REJUVENATE TIRED SKIN WITH A GENTLE LOOFAH RUB..."
HOLIDAY TIPS

"RESTORE INNER HARMONY WITH 45 MINUTES OF MEDITATIVE MUSIC AND YOGA STRETCHES... FOLLOW WITH A 30-MINUTE REVITALIZING YOGURT MASK... A HOT OIL TREATMENT... FRESH MANICURE IN A PERKY HOLIDAY COLOR... AND HOP INTO BED WITH A PIPING MUG OF HERBAL TEA."
HOLIDAY TIPS

...OR SAVE 5½ HOURS BY THROWING OUT THE MAGAZINE AND EATING A BOWL OF POPCORN.
Guisewite

"PUNISHING A DOG AFTER THE FACT IS CONFUSING AND FRUSTRATING FOR THE ANIMAL."
Puppy Training

"THE WORD 'NO' IS ONLY EFFECTIVE IF YOU SAY IT AT THE VERY MOMENT YOUR PUPPY IS DOING SOMETHING WRONG."
Puppy Training

"ONCE YOUR PUPPY KNOWS THE REPERCUSSIONS OF BEING CAUGHT IN THE ACT, SHE WILL QUICKLY LEARN THE KEY TO HAVING A HARMONIOUS LIFE WITH YOU."
Puppy Training

SPEED.
Puppy Training
Guisewite

I'VE SPENT YEARS TRYING TO MAKE IRVING UNDERSTAND WHAT'S ON MY MIND.... HE DOESN'T GET IT.
Happy Holidays

I'VE TALKED, CRIED, DROPPED HINTS, WRITTEN LETTERS, SENT PSYCHIC PLEAS, VISUALIZED, LEFT MESSAGES ON HIS MACHINE AND TYPED UP SUMMARIES IN VERSE.... ZILCH.

YET SOMEHOW HE INSTINCTIVELY KNOWS WHAT I'M GETTING HIM FOR CHRISTMAS, RUNS OUT AND BUYS IT FOR HIMSELF, AND RUINS MY GIFT IDEA.

HOW CAN I BE SO HARD TO UNDERSTAND AND SO EASY TO FIGURE OUT?
Guisewite

YOU CAN'T PARK HERE, CATHY. IT'S ILLEGAL.
OH... I GUESS YOU'RE RIGHT, MOM.
A
C
B
D
F
E
Guisewite

...WAIT A MINUTE! THAT PERSON PARKED IN A SPOT JUST LIKE THE ONE WE JUST PASSED UP! WE COULD HAVE PARKED THERE AFTER ALL!

THE NEXT ILLEGAL SPOT WE SEE IS OURS! FROM NOW ON, ANYTHING GOES! HA, HA! ANY AREA THAT EVEN RESEMBLES A PLACE TO TURN OFF THE MOTOR IS OURS OURS OURS!!

YOU'VE PULLED INTO THE STAIRWELL, DEAR.
I KNOW! CAN YOU BELIEVE OUR LUCK?? JUST CRAWL OUT THE WINDOW, MOM!

9 A.M.... WE'LL HAVE TIME TO GO TO EVERY SINGLE STORE BEFORE THE MALL CLOSES AT 10 P.M....
9 A.M.... WE'LL GET THERE BEFORE IT'S MOBBED...

SPENDING THE DAY SHOPPING FOR OTHERS WILL FILL US WITH THE HOLIDAY SPIRIT, AND BRING US CLOSER THAN EVER BEFORE...
WE'LL SPLIT UP AND FINISH IN HALF THE TIME...

WITH EACH LITTLE DECISION, WE'LL LEARN SPECIAL NEW THINGS ABOUT ONE ANOTHER...
WE'LL ZOOM THROUGH, GRAB THE GIFTS AND MEET BACK AT THE CAR...

THIS WILL BE THE MOST ROMANTIC, MEANINGFUL DAY OF OUR LIVES!!
WE CAN BE OUT OF HERE IN 45 MINUTES!!
Holiday Hours
Guisewite

WHEW! I CAN'T WAIT TO LOOK AT EVERYTHING WE GOT, IRVING!
CATHY, WE JUST SPENT FIVE HOURS AT THE MALL LOOKING AT EVERYTHING WE GOT!

BUT NOW WE HAVE TO SPREAD EVERYTHING OUT AND SEE HOW MUCH WE LIKE IT!
WE BOUGHT IT! WE LIKE IT! DON'T UNWRAP EVERYTHING!
GIFT CENTER

WE HAVE TO RE-EXAMINE EVERYTHING... RETHINK EACH DECISION... COMPARE WHAT WE GOT EVERYONE... DECIDE WHAT TO RETURN....
AAUGH!!

THAT'S THE PROBLEM WITH MEN. THEY THINK SHOPPING IS SUPPOSED TO STOP WHEN YOU LEAVE THE STORE.

MAY I HAVE A BOX FOR THIS?
CERTAINLY. JUST TAKE YOUR RECEIPT TO THE GIFT WRAP DEPARTMENT.
GIFTS

PLEASE... I ALREADY WAITED 35 MINUTES TO BUY IT! I DON'T NEED IT WRAPPED. I JUST WANT THE BOX.
ALL BOXES ARE IN THE GIFT WRAP DEPARTMENT.

EVERYTHING YOU SELL IS A GIFT! EVERY GIFT NEEDS A BOX! YOU HAVE TO HAVE A BOX BACK THERE!!
I HAVE NO BOXES.

FINE. JUST FORGET IT. MAY I HAVE A SHOPPING BAG SO I CAN CARRY IT HOME??
CERTAINLY. JUST GET SOME CHANGE AND GO STAND IN LINE AT THE SHOPPING BAG DISPENSER.

TRY OUR NEW COLOGNE?
NO, THANKS.
For Her

MY BOYFRIEND ALWAYS PICKS OUT A FRAGRANCE HE LOVES FOR ME FOR CHRISTMAS!

THERE'S NOTHING MORE ROMANTIC THAN HAVING THE MAN YOU LOVE CHOOSE THE ONE SPECIAL SCENT THAT HE RESPONDS TO ON HIS MOST PRIMAL, MALE LEVEL...

DON'T YOU WANT TO SMELL IT FIRST, SIR?
NAH... WHATEVER'S ALREADY WRAPPED.

GET OUT OF MY HAND, GUACAMOLE. THIS IS THE OFFICE CHRISTMAS PARTY. I HAVE TO MINGLE!

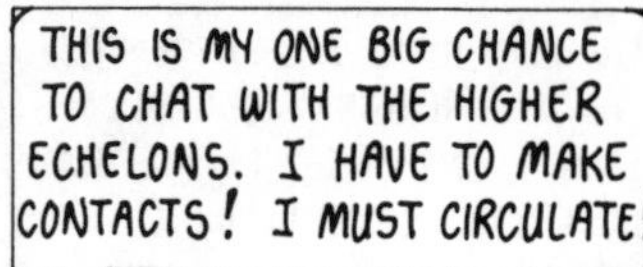
THIS IS MY ONE BIG CHANCE TO CHAT WITH THE HIGHER ECHELONS. I HAVE TO MAKE CONTACTS! I MUST CIRCULATE!

GET OUT OF MY HAND, GUACAMOLE! I AM GOING TO MINGLE! ON THE COUNT OF THREE, YOU ARE TO LEAVE MY HAND SO I CAN MINGLE!!

HOW WAS YOUR BIG PARTY, CATHY?
I GOT STUCK TALKING TO A REAL DIP ALL EVENING.

MY LEFT BRAIN IS MAKING LISTS OF PEOPLE I HAVEN'T SENT CARDS TO YET... MY RIGHT BRAIN IS AT THE CRAFT STORE, THINKING UP CREATIVE GIFTS I COULD STILL MAKE BEFORE SUNDAY...
PINKLEY

MY NERVES ARE AT THE MALL, WORRYING WHETHER I SHOULD HAVE GOTTEN THE OTHER NECKTIE FOR DAD... MY STOMACH IS STILL AT LAST NIGHT'S PARTY, BEGGING FOR MORE CHRISTMAS COOKIES...

...AND MY HEART IS STUCK IN TRAFFIC SOMEWHERE BETWEEN MY MOTHER'S HOUSE, MY BOYFRIEND'S HOUSE AND THE ADORABLE MAN I SAW AT THE POST OFFICE.

WHAT IS IT YOU WANT, CATHY?
MAY WHAT'S LEFT OF ME SNEAK HOME EARLY AND TAKE A NAP?
PINKLEY

DO YOU HAVE ANY OTHER WALLETS?
ALL WE HAVE IS WHAT'S OUT.
Holiday WALLETS

ARE YOU SURE?
NO. YOU'RE RIGHT. WE HAVE A SECRET ROOM IN THE BACK FULL OF GREAT GIFTS WE DON'T WANT ANY OF OUR CUSTOMERS TO SEE.

HAH! I KNEW IT!!
SEE? RIGHT DOWN THIS SECRET HALL AND THROUGH THE SECRET DOOR....

HEY, I'M STANDING IN THE PARKING LOT!! LET ME IN! LET ME BACK IN THE MALL!!
ONE DOWN, 3 MILLION TO GO...

I ACCEPTED IRVING'S INVITATION TO THIS PARTY WITHOUT GRILLING HIM ABOUT WHAT I WAS SUPPOSED TO WEAR.

I DIDN'T ASK WHAT HE WAS WEARING...I DIDN'T MAKE HIM CALL THE HOST...I DIDN'T FORCE HIM TO SNEAK OVER TO THE PARTY EARLY AND PEEK IN THE WINDOW....

FOR ONCE IN MY LIFE, I AM WALKING INTO A SITUATION EXUDING CONFIDENCE AND NONCHALANCE!!

HI!
I HAVE TO GO HOME AND CHANGE CLOTHES.
I KNEW IT WAS TOO GOOD TO BE TRUE.

IF YOU DON'T LIKE IT, YOU CAN EXCHANGE IT, IRVING. PLEASE BE HONEST.

IF YOU'D RATHER HAVE ANOTHER COLOR, FINE! IF YOU WANT SOMETHING ELSE, FINE! I JUST WANT YOU TO BE HAPPY!

MY FEELINGS WON'T BE HURT. IT'S JUST A TOKEN! THE ACTUAL ITEM DOESN'T MATTER! ALL THAT COUNTS IS THAT YOU'RE HAPPY! I JUST WANT YOU TO BE HAPPY!!

THANKS, CATHY. WELL... MAYBE WE'LL JUST GO BACK AND SEE WHAT ELSE IS...
WAAHH!!

VACUUM THE CARPET! MOP THE FLOOR! WASH THE CURTAINS! I WANT EVERYTHING TO BE PERFECT FOR CATHY'S VISIT!

POLISH THE CHINA! SCRUB THE WINDOWS! REDECORATE THE BATHROOM! IT HAS TO BE PERFECT!!
TOOLS

PAINT THE CEILINGS! RECOVER THE SOFA! WALLPAPER THE KITCHEN! CLEAN OUT THE CUPBOARDS! IT HAS TO BE PERFECT! EVERYTHING HAS TO BE PERFECT!!

HI, MOM AND DAD! OH, THE HOUSE LOOKS JUST AS I REMEMBERED IT!
PERFECT...
PAINT

I CAN'T BELIEVE WE'RE INTO THE CHRISTMAS CAKE AGAIN, CATHY.
DON'T BE SO HARD ON YOURSELF, MOM.

WE PROMISED OURSELVES WE WOULDN'T EAT ANY MORE CAKE.
MOM, IT'S THE DAY AFTER CHRISTMAS. YOU'RE SUPPOSED TO EAT CAKE!

ALL OVER THE COUNTRY, FAMILIES ARE RELAXING TOGETHER EATING CAKE!

DO YOU THINK MOST FAMILIES ARE AT IT BEFORE BREAKFAST?
OK, FINE. WE'RE OVERACHIEVERS.

MOM, WE ONLY HAD COFFEE AND TOAST. HOW CAN IT TAKE TWO HOURS TO CLEAN THE KITCHEN??
I WANTED TO MAKE SURE THE CUPS WERE RINSED OUT, CATHY.

YOU'VE SPENT LONGER CLEANING UP BREAKFAST THAN I'VE SPENT IN MY KITCHEN IN THE LAST MONTH!
FINE. IF YOU'RE ALL DRESSED, I'LL BE OUT IN A MINUTE.

DRESSED? I'M NOT DRESSED! I JUST GOT MY HAIR DRIED!
YOU'VE SPENT LONGER DRYING YOUR HAIR THAN I'VE SPENT ON MY ENTIRE BODY IN THE LAST MONTH!

EVEN WHEN WE'RE SLEEPING UNDER THE SAME ROOF, WE'RE LIVING IN DIFFERENT TIME ZONES...

YOUR PUPPY JUST MADE A MESS ON THE FLOOR.
SHE NEVER DOES THAT! SHE'S NEVER LIKE THAT! SHE'S JUST NERVOUS AROUND COMPANY!!

YOUR DAUGHTER JUST GAVE HER A COOKIE!
SHE NEVER DOES THAT! SHE'S NEVER LIKE THAT! SHE'S JUST NERVOUS AROUND COMPANY!!

WE COME FROM A LONG LINE OF DENIAL.

HOW'S YOUR PUPPY, ELECTRA, CATHY?
OH, SHE'S SO CUTE! SHE SLEEPS WITH HER HEAD RIGHT ON THE PILLOW NEXT TO MINE!
COFFEE ROOM RULES

MY CAT DOES THE SAME THING. SHE JUST SORT OF NUZZLES ME TO WAKE ME UP!
WHEN I WAKE UP, ELECTRA HAS HER ARM AROUND MY NECK AS IF SHE'S BEEN HUGGING ME ALL NIGHT!

SIGH.

REMEMBER WHEN WE USED TO TALK ABOUT MEN THIS WAY?
DON'T GET ME STARTED, CHARLENE...
Guisewite

I'VE BEEN INVOLVED IN HUNDREDS OF EXCITING PROJECTS ALL YEAR.... AT MY MOTHER'S HOUSE, I SLUMP ON THE COUCH AND WATCH TV.

I'VE TRAVELED, READ, LEARNED, GROWN.... AT MOM'S HOUSE, I SLUMP ON THE COUCH AND WATCH TV.

I'VE ELEVATED MY PERSPECTIVE AND EXPANDED MY VISION IN A THOUSAND WAYS.... AT MOM'S HOUSE, I SLUMP ON THE COUCH AND WATCH TV.

I BROUGHT HOME A WHOLE NEW MENTAL WARDROBE, BUT ALL I EVER LET HER SEE IS MY MENTAL SWEATSUIT.

MOM, DON'T BRING OUT A PLATTER OF COLD CUTS. WE JUST FINISHED LUNCH.
I THOUGHT ELECTRA MIGHT WANT A LITTLE SNACK.

ELECTRA'S SUPPOSED TO EAT ONLY PUPPY FOOD.
I'LL JUST PUT IT HERE IN CASE ANYONE GETS HUNGRY.
NO ONE'S GOING TO GET HUNGRY.

NO ONE WANTS ANY MORE FOOD! NO ONE'S GOING TO EAT IT! NO ONE'S GOING TO TOUCH IT! PLEASE! PUT THE FOOD AWAY!!

EVEN WHEN I KNOW THEY'LL HATE ME FOR IT, IT MAKES ME FEEL GOOD TO SEE THEM EAT.

BY 9:30, EVERYONE WILL HAVE SEEN HOW I LOOK IN THIS SKIN-TIGHT DRESS, AND I CAN START NIBBLING ON THE HORS D'OEUVRES...

BY 10:00, THE ROOM WILL BE SO CROWDED, NO ONE WILL BE ABLE TO GET A FULL VIEW OF ME, AND I CAN BEGIN SOME SERIOUS EATING....

BY 11:15, NO ONE WILL BE AWARE OF ANYTHING, AND I CAN MOVE INTO A CALORIC FREE-FOR-ALL!!

IF MEN ONLY KNEW THE SECRET PLANS OF PASSION A WOMAN HAS ON NEW YEAR'S EVE....

DON'T LEAVE, CATHY! DON'T LEAVE SO SOON!!
MOM, THE HOLIDAYS ARE OVER. I HAVE TO GO BACK TO WORK.

WE HARDLY EVER SEE YOU! LITTLE ELECTRA IS GROWING UP SO FAST!
I ALREADY STAYED FOUR DAYS LONGER THAN I PLANNED.

YOU NEED MORE FOOD! YOU NEED MORE REST! YOU'RE JUST A BABY!!
FINE. YOU CALL MY BOSS AND EXPLAIN IT TO HIM.

MR. PINKLEY WON'T BE IN TODAY. HIS MOTHER WON'T LET HIM OUT OF HIS BEDROOM.

NO, ELECTRA. NO COOKIES TONIGHT. I'M ON MY NEW YEAR'S DIET.

OH, THAT'S NOT FAIR, IS IT? YOU'RE NOT ON A DIET. YOU COULD HAVE A LITTLE PIECE OF COOKIE.

HERE, ELECTRA...MOMMY WILL HELP YOU. MOMMY WILL GET RID OF ALL THE BIG, ICKY PIECES THAT MIGHT MAKE YOU SICK! MOMMY WON'T LET YOU CHOKE!! MOMMY WILL SAVE YOU!!!

COOKIES

SOMETIMES I ASTOUND EVEN MYSELF.
COOKIES

I HAVE A GREAT IDEA FOR TONIGHT, CATHY.
IRVING, I HAVE TO GO TO MY HEALTH CLUB. REMEMBER?? I'M ON MY WHOLE NEW PROGRAM!

GO TOMORROW.
THIS IS THE CRITICAL DAY NUMBER TWO! IF I DON'T GO TODAY, THE WHOLE YEAR IS RUINED!!

I'M WORKING OUT EVERY SINGLE NIGHT AND EATING ONLY SMALL GREEN SALADS UNTIL I LOSE 23 POUNDS AND REACH TONED PERFECTION IN EVERY MUSCLE GROUP! NOW, GET OUT OF HERE SO I CAN GET READY!!

WHY IS IT THAT INDULGING HER WOMANLY FANTASIES ALWAYS REQUIRES ME LEAVING THE HOUSE?

SHOULDN'T WE HAVE WARNED CATHY WE WERE DROPPING OFF SOME THINGS SHE LEFT AT OUR HOUSE?
IF WE WARN HER, SHE JUST OVER-PREPARES AND CLAMS UP, DEAR.
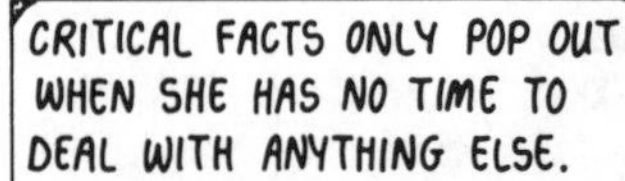
CRITICAL FACTS ONLY POP OUT WHEN SHE HAS NO TIME TO DEAL WITH ANYTHING ELSE.

DING DONG!

BLIND DATE. LAWYER. 35. NEVER MARRIED. SOUNDS CUTE. SEEING "ACCIDENTAL TOURIST". WINNER, "NEW YORK FILM CRITICS, BEST PICTURE OF YEAR". MEETING FOR CHINESE FIRST. IRVING DOESN'T KNOW. BYE.

THE "CLIFF NOTES" APPROACH TO MOTHERHOOD.
Guisewite

THIS IS SO BEAUTIFUL... SO TOUCHING...SO SAD... SO ROMANTIC....
POP CORN
POP CORN
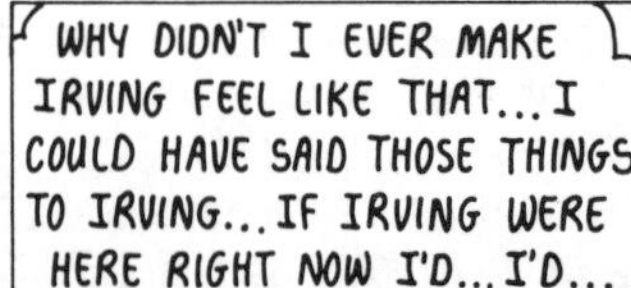
WHY DIDN'T I EVER MAKE IRVING FEEL LIKE THAT... I COULD HAVE SAID THOSE THINGS TO IRVING... IF IRVING WERE HERE RIGHT NOW I'D... I'D...

EXIT
EXIT

GREAT SHOW, HUH?
I DON'T WANT TO TALK ABOUT IT!!

NOW SHOWING
THE ACCIDENTA TOURIST

THERE'S NOTHING WORSE THAN SEEING THE RIGHT MOVIE WITH THE WRONG MAN.
Guisewite

HI, CATHY. UM... I JUST CALLED TO SEE HOW YOU LIKED THE MOVIE.
MOVIE?

WEREN'T YOU GOING TO SEE A MOVIE??
OH, YEAH. "ACCIDENTAL TOURIST". I LOVED IT, MOM. IT'S A GREAT MOVIE.
... AND YOUR BLIND DATE?? ... DIDN'T YOU MENTION A BLIND DATE??
UM, HM. MY DATE LOVED THE MOVIE, TOO.

ANYTHING ELSE YOU WANT TO SHARE WITH YOUR MOTHER??
NO, NOT REALLY.

I GOT THE WORDS "LOVED" AND "DATE" IN THE SAME SENTENCE, BUT I THINK IT WOULD BE STRETCHING IT TO SAY THEY'RE RELATED.
Guisewite

I'VE EATEN A HALF-GALLON OF ICE CREAM AT ONE SITTING.
DIET DIARY
VOL. V DIET
VOL. IV DIET
VOL. III DIET
VOL. II DIET
VOL. I DIET

I'VE HAD NOTHING BUT VEGETABLE JUICE ALL DAY AND THEN EATEN NINE BROWNIES FIVE MINUTES BEFORE GOING TO BED... I'VE EATEN A CHEESECAKE FOR DINNER, AND WASHED IT DOWN WITH MELTED SQUARES OF BAKING CHOCOLATE.

YET I HESITATE TO TRY THE NEW LIQUID DIET BECAUSE IT MIGHT NOT BE GOOD FOR ME.
diet soda

WHY DOES MY COMMON SENSE ONLY KICK IN WHEN IT HEARS ABOUT SOMETHING THAT COULD MAKE ME THIN?
diet soda

ARE YOU OK, CATHY?
I'VE HIT THE 130-POUND PLATEAU AGAIN, IRVING.

I GET HERE EVERY YEAR. IT COMES RIGHT BEFORE THE VALLEY OF THE 120s, WHICH I SAW FOR 15 MINUTES IN 1984... WHICH IS RIGHT BEFORE THE 110s, WHICH I'VE NEVER VISITED, BUT HAVE PICTURES OF PLASTERED ALL OVER MY REFRIGERATOR.

SOMEHOW I ALWAYS MISS THE EXIT TO THE 120s, ZOOM BACK UP TO THE ROLLING HILLS OF THE 130s, AND GET STALLED OUT IN THE DREADED CAVE OF DOOM, THE 140s.

MY BODY IS LESS LIKE A TEMPLE, AND MORE LIKE A TOUR BUS.

WE'RE PERFECT, CATHY. WE HAVE THE SOLID FOUNDATION OF GROWING UP IN THE '50s... THE SOCIAL COMPASSION OF COMING OF AGE IN THE '60s...

THE FREE SPIRITS OF BEING YOUNG ADULTS IN THE '70s... COMBINED WITH THE RESPONSIBLE CITIZENSHIP OF THE '80s...

DON'T YOU SEE WHAT THAT MAKES US??

OLD.
PASS THE RETIN-A.

AREN'T YOU COMING TO THE HEALTH CLUB, CATHY?
I CAN'T. I HAVE TO TAKE CARE OF THIS KLINE MESS TONIGHT.

THEN I HAVE TO GET TO THE COOPER PROBLEM, THE BLAKE CRISIS... AND I TOLD JOHN I'D HELP HIM OUT WITH THE HARLAN FIASCO.

YOU VOLUNTEERED FOR EXTRA WORK ON TOP OF ALL THAT??
EVERY SERIOUS PROFESSIONAL LIVES BY THE SAME SIMPLE RULE, CHARLENE.

IT'S EASIER TO FACE 25 DISASTERS THAN ONE LEOTARD.
Guisewite

HOW COULD I DO THIS TO MYSELF?? I WAS ACTUALLY LOSING SOME WEIGHT! I WAS ACTUALLY MAKING PROGRESS!!

BUT IN THE LAST 24 HOURS, I GOT DISCOURAGED, HIT THE BAKERY, AND UNDID THREE MONTHS OF WORK! HOW COULD I DO THIS TO MYSELF?!

COME ON, CATHY. YOU'LL ONLY START MAKING PROGRESS AGAIN IF YOU CAN REFOCUS ON A MORE POSITIVE THOUGHT.

HOW CAN I BLAME THIS ON SOMEONE ELSE??
OOPS. LOOK AT THE TIME. I SHOULD BE RUNNING ALONG.
Guisewite

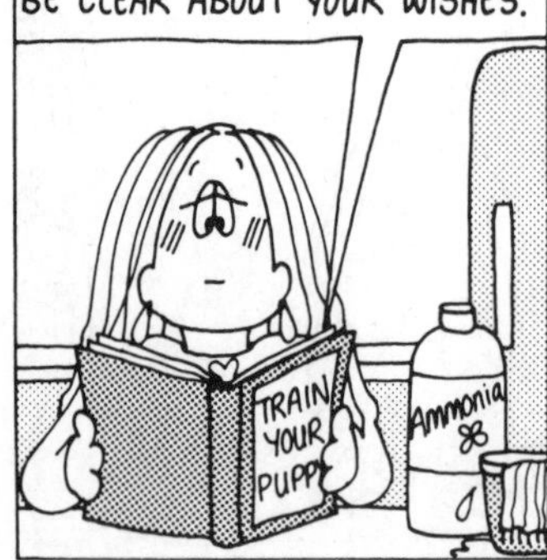
"IF YOUR PUPPY IS NOT HOUSEBROKEN AFTER TWO MONTHS OF TRYING, YOU ARE FAILING TO BE CLEAR ABOUT YOUR WISHES."
TRAIN YOUR PUPPY
Ammonia

"AS IN ALL OTHER KINDS OF TRAINING, HOUSEBREAKING CAN HAPPEN ONLY WHEN YOU GIVE FIRM, EXACTING GUIDELINES FOR WHAT IS ACCEPTABLE."
TRAIN YOUR PUPP

"MANY PET OWNERS NOTICE DRAMATIC IMPROVEMENT BY INCORPORATING ONE SIMPLE KEY PHRASE INTO THE TRAINING COMMAND STRUCTURE."
TRAIN YOUR PUPPY

MOVE OVER.
DOG TREATS
ELECTRA
ICE CREAM
Guisewite

AACK! THOSE ARE MY NEW SUEDE PUMPS! YOU'RE EATING MY NEW SUEDE PUMPS!!

ELECTRA, A WOMAN'S SHOES ARE SACRED! A WOMAN'S SHOES ARE HER LIFE! YOU ARE NEVER, NEVER, NEVER TO GET YOUR POINTY LITTLE TEETH NEAR A PAIR OF WOMAN'S SHOES!!!

BOOTS!

YOU DIDN'T HAVE ANY TROUBLE HOUSEBREAKING YOUR PUPPY, DID YOU, CATHY?
ME? OH, WELL, I...

OUR LITTLE SNUGGLES WAS HOUSEBROKEN THE SECOND DAY!
ELECTRA LEARNED QUICKLY, TOO!
WE CORRECTED HER ONCE AND THEN SHE JUST KNEW!
ELECTRA KNEW WITHOUT ME EVER TELLING HER!

WE CAN LEAVE HER FOR HOURS AND SHE'D NEVER MAKE A MISTAKE!!
ELECTRA NOT ONLY WAITS ALL DAY, BUT INSISTS THAT I TAKE A NICE HOT SHOWER AFTER WORK BEFOR TAKING HER OUT! HAH!!

CROSS MELINDA OFF THE LIST OF PEOPLE WHO WILL EVER BE ALLOWED NEAR MY LIVING ROOM CARPET.

"REWARDING YOUR PUPPY WITH TREATS WILL ONLY LEAD TO OBESITY AND BEGGING."
TRAIN YOUR PUPPY

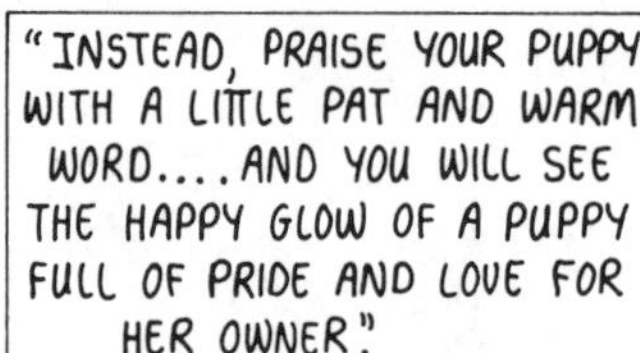
"INSTEAD, PRAISE YOUR PUPPY WITH A LITTLE PAT AND WARM WORD.... AND YOU WILL SEE THE HAPPY GLOW OF A PUPPY FULL OF PRIDE AND LOVE FOR HER OWNER."

TRAIN YOUR PUPPY

GOOD GIRL, ELECTRA!
TRAIN YOUR PUPPY

WHERE'S THE FOOD?

I THINK I'LL GO SEE HOW CATHY'S DOING WITH LITTLE ELECTRA.
CATHY WILL SCREAM IF YOU BRING HER ANY MORE CLIPPINGS ON HOW TO HOUSEBREAK A PUPPY.

I'M NOT BRINGING ANY HOUSE-BREAKING CLIPPINGS.
SHE DOESN'T WANT ANY MORE SPEECHES. NO TIPS. NO HINTS. NO LECTURES.

BELIEVE ME, DEAR. I UNDERSTAND THE SENSITIVITIES OF GROWN CHILDREN WITH LITTLE ONES OF THEIR OWN!!

THEY'LL TURN AWAY A MOTHER FULL OF ADVICE, BUT THEY'LL NEVER SAY NO TO ONE HOLDING A MOP.

MOST SHOPPERS MAKE THEIR CHRISTMAS RETURNS THE DAY AFTER CHRISTMAS. IT'S A BIG HELP TO THE STORE OWNERS.

SOME WAIT UNTIL THE FIRST WEEK OF THE NEW YEAR SO THEY CAN CASH IN ON THE HOTTEST SALES.

THIS WEEK, AS WE CELEBRATE THE ONE-MONTH ANNIVERSARY OF CHRISTMAS, WE SEE THOSE SPECIAL INDIVIDUALS WHO ARE MOTIVATED BY SOMETHING EVEN LARGER THAN ALTRUISM AND GOOD BARGAINS....

...THE ONES WHO JUST GOT THEIR CHARGE CARD STATEMENTS FOR DECEMBER.

AACK! I MEANT TO RETURN ALL THIS STUFF! IT'S COMING BACK!! I SWEAR! STOP THE FINANCE CHARGES!

I TRIED THIS DRESS ON AT THE STORE FIVE TIMES ON THREE SEPARATE DAYS IN EARLY DECEMBER.

I BROUGHT IT HOME, TRIED IT ON 22 MORE TIMES DURING THE NEXT SIX WEEKS, AND SPENT A WHOLE EVENING MODELING IT WITH EVERYTHING IN MY CLOSET.

ALTHOUGH I'VE HAD THE DRESS ON 27 TIMES, PAID FOR IT, AND SHOWN IT TO EVERYONE I KNOW, IT HAS NOT TECHNICALLY BEEN "WORN," AND COULD BE RETURNED.

EVERYONE THINKS WE'RE MARRIED AND I'M STILL TRYING TO DECIDE WHETHER OR NOT I WANT TO GO OUT.

THE SALESWOMAN SPENT 45 MINUTES HELPING ME WHILE I AGONIZED OVER WHETHER TO GET THIS DRESS...

SHE COMPLIMENTED ME, ENCOURAGED ME, AND CHEERFULLY HUNG UP THE 17 OTHER OUTFITS I HAD TO TRY ON BEFORE I COULD MAKE A DECISION.

NOW I'M DRIVING 30 MILES OUT OF MY WAY SO I CAN RETURN IT AT A DIFFERENT BRANCH OF THE STORE SO I WON'T HAVE TO SEE HER FACE.

THERE'S NO LIMIT TO HOW FAR WE'LL GO TO AVOID SOMEONE WHO'S BEEN GOOD TO US.

HELLO, CATHY. WE'VE BEEN EXPECTING YOU.
I BEG YOUR PARDON?
Fashions fo

THE SALESCLERK AT THE STORE ACROSS TOWN WARNED US YOU'D TRY TO SNEAK IN HERE AND RETURN CLOTHES YOU BOUGHT BEFORE CHRISTMAS.
ME? AHEM, I....

WHEN YOU WALK IN ANY OF OUR BRANCHES, A BUZZER SOUNDS, ALERTING ALL CLERKS TO PREPARE TO RETALLY OUR CHRISTMAS TOTALS!
OH. AHEM.. ..I WASN'T RETURNING THIS...

SHOE DEPARTMENTS IN FIVE STATES HAVE BEEN WARNED ABOUT THE TWO PAIRS OF "BACK-UP" NEW YEAR'S EVE PUMPS YOU'RE STILL TRYING TO UNLOAD.
Guisewite

IT'S SO EMBARRASSING TO RETURN THINGS THIS LONG AFTER CHRISTMAS, MOM.
I HAVE THINGS FROM CHRISTMAS 1958, THAT I NEVER GOT AROUND TO RETURNING.

I HATE FACING THE SALES-CLERKS.
I ONCE TOOK A CROSS-COUNTRY TRIP SO I COULD RETURN THINGS WHERE THEY'D NEVER KNOW ME.
Guisewite

YOU DID??
I ONCE PAID A TOTAL STRANGER $25 TO SNEAK INTO A STORE AND RETURN A PAIR OF $19 GLOVES!

REALLY?? HA, HA!! YOU'RE WORSE THAN I AM! HA!
SOMETIMES THE KINDEST THING WE CAN DO FOR OUR CHILDREN IS TO SET A BAD EXAMPLE.

HI.
I PAID ONLY $39 FOR THIS JACKET, IRVING!!

IT'S VERY NICE.
IT WAS MY SHOPPING SCORE OF THE YEAR! LOOK! $400...MARKED DOWN TO $285... SLASHED TO $177... CHOPPED TO $98... CUT TO $39!!!

A $400 JACKET FOR $39!! NO ONE WOULD EVER KNOW! NO ONE COULD EVER SUSPECT THE DEAL I GOT! HA, HA!! MY SECRET TRIUMPH!

HI.
I PAID ONLY $39 FOR THIS JACKET!!
Guisewite

FEVER, SORE THROAT, UPSET STOMACH... IT SOUNDS LIKE THE COMBINATION FLU-COLD THAT EVERYONE'S BEEN GETTING.

JUST STAY IN BED AND RIDE IT OUT, CATHY.

I'M AFRAID NO DOCTOR IN THE WORLD KNOWS THE ONE ANSWER THAT MIGHT MAKE YOU FEEL BETTER.

HOW MUCH WEIGHT MIGHT I LOSE?

CATHY, YOU'RE SICK. WHAT ARE YOU DOING HERE??
I WANTED TO LOCK MY DESK SO YOU COULDN'T SNOOP THROUGH IT WHILE I'M ON MY DEATH BED, CHARLENE.
RECEPTIONIST

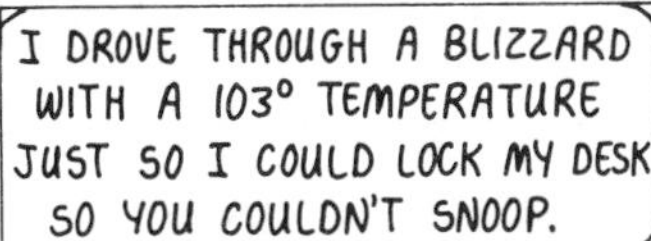
I DROVE THROUGH A BLIZZARD WITH A 103° TEMPERATURE JUST SO I COULD LOCK MY DESK SO YOU COULDN'T SNOOP.

CATHY

I CAN'T BELIEVE THIS, CATHY! YOU'RE MY BEST FRIEND! I CAN'T BELIEVE YOU DON'T KNOW ME BETTER THAN THAT!
SORRY, CHARLENE.

DOES SHE ACTUALLY THINK I DON'T HAVE A COPY OF HER KEY?
I CHANGED THE LOCK LAST MONTH.

Yap Yap
ISN'T THAT CUTE? YOU KNOW I'M SICK, ELECTRA, AND YOU WANT TO HELP.

Yap Yap Yap
YOU'RE SO WORRIED. YOU'RE SO SWEET. OH, IT'S MOMENTS LIKE THIS THAT A MOTHER LIVES FOR!!

Yap Yap Yap Yap Yap Yap

...AND IT'S MOMENTS LIKE THIS WHEN SHE RE-THINKS THE WHOLE DEAL.

DELIRIOUS WITH FEVER, SHE STAGGERS INTO THE BATHROOM AND PUTS ON EYELINER JUST IN CASE HER SWEETHEART DECIDES TO STOP OVER WITH SOME NICE, HOT SOUP...

HEAD THROBBING, STOMACH REELING, LUNGS CRACKING, SHE MANAGES TO TRY ON EVERY NIGHTGOWN UNTIL SHE FINDS THE MOST FLATTERING, JUST IN CASE HER SWEETIE DECIDES TO SURPRISE HER WITH SOME GET-WELL FLOWERS...

...IRVING??
WILL YOU CALL MY DOCTOR, CATHY? I HAVE A LITTLE SORE THROAT.

MUSCLES ACHING, SHE SOMEHOW FINDS THE STRENGTH TO REARRANGE HER PHOTO ALBUM OF HER LOVED ONE....

BLEAH!

DO YOU HAVE ANYTHING TO TAKE FOR YOUR COLD, IRVING?
SURE. IN THE REFRIGERATOR I HAVE..UM...SOME OLD RIBS, AND IN THE MEDICINE CABINET I HAVE.. ....UH... SOME AFTER-SHAVE.
Tissues

THAT'S TERRIBLE!! HOW CAN A GROWN MAN BE SO TOTALLY UNPREPARED TO CARE FOR HIMSELF?!
WHAT DO YOU HAVE FOR YOUR COLD?

DIET COKE AND SIX KINDS OF CREME RINSE.
diet
diet

MY MOTHER, A SELF-SACRIFICING HOUSEWIFE, NEVER LET HAVING THE FLU COME BEFORE THE NEEDS OF HER FAMILY.

I'M WEARING AN OXYGEN MASK SO I WON'T GET GERMS ON THE BREAD I'M BAKING.

OXYGEN

I, A DYNAMIC CAREER WOMAN, FLOP INTO BED AND LEAVE PATHETIC MESSAGES ON ALL MY FRIENDS' ANSWERING MACHINES AT THE FIRST SIGN OF A SNIFFLE.

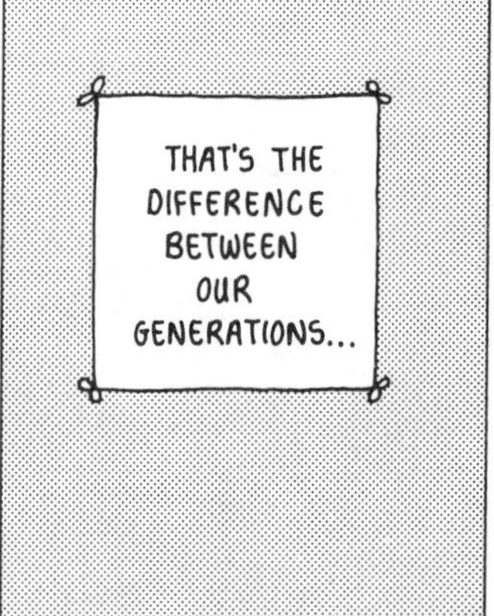

THAT'S THE DIFFERENCE BETWEEN OUR GENERATIONS...

WOMEN TODAY HAVE SO MUCH MORE SELF-RESPECT.

I'M SICK. I CAN'T BREATHE! FAX ME SOME SOUP!

EVEN WHEN MY BABY IS 20 MILES AWAY WITH A BABY SITTER ALL DAY, I KNOW EXACTLY WHAT SHE'S DOING.
ME, TOO.

MY LITTLE NICOLE IS HAVING HER JUICE BOTTLE RIGHT NOW!
MY LITTLE JACOB IS JUST WAKING UP FROM HIS NAP!

MY LITTLE MEGAN IS ALL CURLED UP WATCHING HER "E.T." TAPE!
MY LITTLE NOAH IS PLAYING WITH HIS RED TRUCK!

MY LITTLE PUPPY IS DOING SOMETHING REALLY HIDEOUS INVOLVING THE LIVING ROOM CARPET.
Guisewite

WOMEN TODAY SEE THE VALENTINE INDUSTRY FOR THE COMMERCIALIZED HYPE THAT IT IS.
GET REAL.
My Darling
Photos
TO MY LOVE

WE DO NOT MEASURE OUR SELF-WORTH BY WHETHER OR NOT WE GET A VALENTINE.
WHO DESIGNS THIS? WHO DO THEY THINK WANTS THIS??
My Darling
Valentine Paper Towels

IN FACT, FOR MANY WOMEN, ONLY ONE OTHER EVENT ALL YEAR INSPIRES SUCH FEELINGS OF TOTAL, UTTER INDIGNATION.

VALENTINE'S DAY: BATHING SUIT SEASON FOR THE HEART.
AND WHERE'S THE ONE FOR ME??!
Photos
Guisewite

I SIT AT HOME AND WAIT FOR FRANKIE TO CALL, CATHY.

I THINK ABOUT HIM... WONDER ABOUT HIM... WORRY ABOUT HIM...
diet

I SPREAD OUT ALL OUR OLD PICTURES AND RELIVE EVERY MINUTE I'VE SPENT WITH HIM.
diet

I'M NOT HAVING A RELATIONSHIP. I'M HAVING A VIGIL.
Guisewite

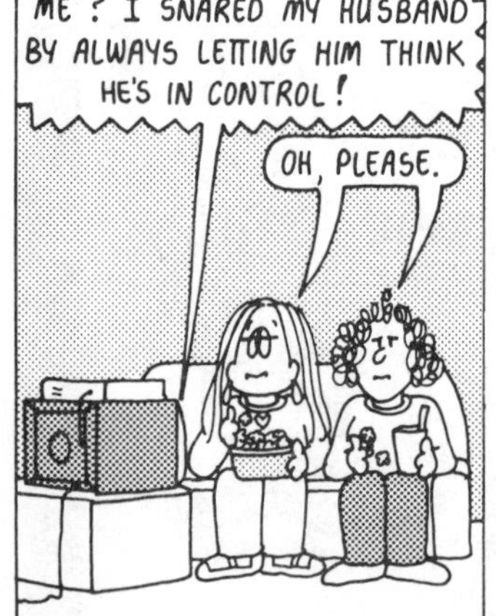
ME? I SNARED MY HUSBAND BY ALWAYS LETTING HIM THINK HE'S IN CONTROL!
OH, PLEASE.

HE THINKS HE'S IN CONTROL... EVERYONE ELSE THINKS HE'S IN CONTROL... BUT DEEP DOWN, I KNOW I'M REALLY THE ONE IN CONTROL BECAUSE I LET HIM ACT LIKE HE'S IN CONTROL!
I'M GOING TO BE SICK.

AFTER SIX MONTHS OF LETTING HIM FEEL TOTALLY IN CONTROL, HE FELL TO HIS KNEES LAST VALENTINE'S DAY AND BEGGED ME TO MARRY HIM! HE ACTUALLY THOUGHT IT WAS ALL HIS IDEA! HA, HA!!

WHILE I'M IN THE BATHROOM THROWING UP, WRITE DOWN WHERE TO ORDER HER BOOK.
Guisewite

WHAT ARE YOU GETTING CATHY FOR VALENTINE'S DAY, IRVING ?
VALENTINE'S DAY ??

WHO KNOWS ? IT'S SO FAR OFF. I DIDN'T THINK ABOUT IT YET.

I DON'T EVEN KNOW IF SHE'D EXPECT ANYTHING THIS YEAR !

Valentine's Day Countdown
TO DO BEFORE FEB 14
HAIR APPT.
MAKEOVER
NAILS
REDECORATE
LOSE 10 lbs.
5
SHOPPING DAYS
Guide to Romance

WHY SHOULD I LISTEN TO YOUR TIPS FOR VALENTINE'S DAY, CHARLENE ?

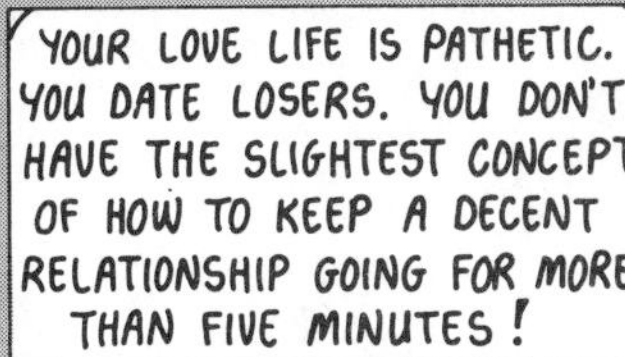
YOUR LOVE LIFE IS PATHETIC. YOU DATE LOSERS. YOU DON'T HAVE THE SLIGHTEST CONCEPT OF HOW TO KEEP A DECENT RELATIONSHIP GOING FOR MORE THAN FIVE MINUTES !

FINE. WHY NOT ASK YOUR MOTHER FOR TIPS? SHE'S BEEN HAPPILY MARRIED TO A WONDERFUL MAN FOR 40 YEARS.

SORRY. WHAT WAS I THINKING ?
NOW, FOR THE VALENTINE'S DAY WARDROBE, I RECOMMEND....

PERFECT. I'LL GET THIS FOR IRVING FOR VALENTINE'S DAY !
YOU CAN'T. IT'S TOO EXPENSIVE. TOO INTENSE.
FOR HIM
WATCHES

I'LL GET THIS FOR IRVING !
TOO THREATENING.
I'LL GET THIS AND THIS AND THIS !
TOO SERIOUS. TOO SHOWY. TOO PERSONAL.

I'LL BUY IT ALL ! I'LL FILL HIS HOME WITH PRESENTS !
FINE. SCARE HIM OFF. DRIVE HIM AWAY. YOU CAN START GOING OUT TO DINNER WITH ME AGAIN.

WHAT DID YOU DECIDE TO GET FOR IRVING ?
THE GIFT OF RESTRAINT.

MY WORST WAS THE VALENTINE'S DAY I SPENT $200 ON LINGERIE... WAS TOO EMBARRASSED TO LET MY DATE IN THE FRONT DOOR... AND THEN SULKED FOR A MONTH BECAUSE HE DIDN'T RESPOND TO THE SEDUCTION HE NEVER KNEW I WAS TRYING...

I ONCE BAKED A VALENTINE CAKE FOR MY DATE... GOT NERVOUS... ATE THE WHOLE THING BEFORE HE GOT THERE AND THEN WOULDN'T LET HIM TOUCH ME BECAUSE I FELT SO FAT!

HA, HA! I SPENT SO LONG PREPARING A ROMANTIC SPEECH THAT I STARTED SOBBING HYSTERICALLY WHEN I TRIED TO GIVE IT AND THEN BROKE UP WITH MY BOYFRIEND BECAUSE HE COULDN'T GUESS WHAT WAS WRONG!

ATTENTION MEN OF THE WORLD: GET YOUR BUS TICKETS OUT OF TOWN WHILE YOU STILL HAVE A CHANCE.

ATTENTION ALL EMPLOYEES: BEAUTIFUL, ROMANTIC, VALENTINE BOUQUETS HAVE ARRIVED FOR DIANE, DONNA, ELENA, JOHN, BOB, PEGGY, TOM, JIM, DENISE, DOROTHY, LEE, JAKE, GEORGE, BARBARA AND JEAN.
RECEPTIONIST

ALL OTHERS ARE INVITED TO JOIN ME IN THE CONFERENCE ROOM TO FOCUS ON THE REAL BUSINESS OF THE DAY.
RECEPTIONIST

RECEPTIONIST

BRING YOUR OWN SPOON.
PTIONIST
ICE CREAM

WHAT HAPPENED WITH IRVING, CATHY? HOW WAS VALENTINE'S NIGHT??
NICE, THANKS.
RECEPTIONIST

"NICE"?? THAT'S ALL I GET? "NICE"?!
I DON'T TELL YOU EVERYTHING, CHARLENE.
CATHY

YOU TELL ME ALL THE BAD STUFF! I GET INSTANT REPLAYS OF THE HIDEOUS TIMES! I'VE COUNSELED YOU... COMFORTED YOU... IF YOU'VE HAD A GOOD DATE, I WANT FACTS! YOU OWE ME DETAILS!!!
IT WAS VERY NICE.
CATH

I'M STARTING TO KNOW WHAT IT FEELS LIKE TO BE HER MOTHER.
CATHY

AT THE OFFICE, I'M TOUGH! ENERGIZED! DYNAMIC! DECISIVE! EFFICIENT! IN CONTROL!

WHEN I GET HOME, I SPEND THE EVENING WANDERING IN AND OUT OF THE KITCHEN, NIBBLING ON LITTLE BITS OF FOOD.
Snack Crackers
Chips

POP CORN
diet

WHAT HAPPENS ON THE FREEWAY THAT TRANSFORMS ME FROM SUPERWOMAN TO MINNIE MOUSE?
diet

I'LL GET UP EARLY TOMORROW AND WORK ON THIS REPORT.... I'LL GET UP REALLY EARLY AND GO TO THE HEALTH CLUB BEFORE I WORK ON THIS REPORT....

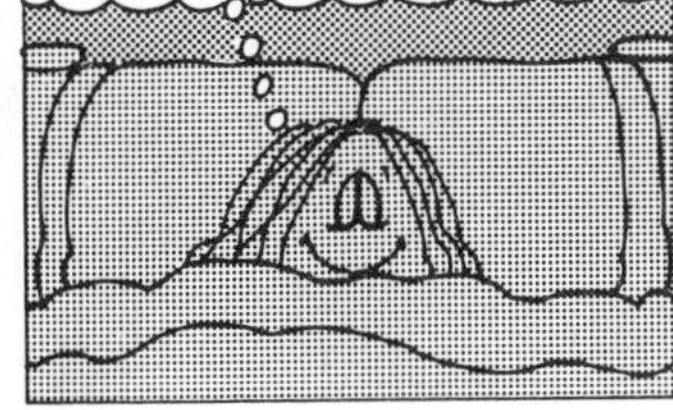
I'LL GET UP REALLY, REALLY EARLY AND PAY BILLS BEFORE I GO TO THE HEALTH CLUB.... I'LL GET UP EXTREMELY EARLY AND DO THE LAUNDRY BEFORE I PAY BILLS BEFORE I GO TO THE HEALTH CLUB BEFORE I WORK ON THAT REPORT.....

AACK! 7:00!! I WAS SUPPOSED TO BE UP AT 3:15!! I'M FINISHED! I'M RUINED! AAACK!!
BRIIING!!

NOT MANY PEOPLE COULD FALL A WHOLE WEEK BEHIND BY WAKING UP AT THEIR NORMAL TIME.
7:00

CALL ME, IRVING...MISS ME.. ..NEED ME...THINK ABOUT HOW MUCH YOU WANT TO SEE ME....
CATHY

RING RING

CATHY, PLEASE COME TO MY OFFICE RIGHT AWAY! I NEED YOU! I MUST SEE YOU RIGHT NOW! PLEASE!

HOW QUICKLY WE GO FROM BEING TELEPATHIC TO BEING TELEPATHETIC.

DOES IRVING KNOW HOW TO MAKE YOU LAUGH?
YES!
DOES HE KNOW HOW TO MAKE YOU FEEL GOOD ABOUT YOURSELF?
YES!

DOES HE KNOW HOW TO SHARE SPECIAL, TENDER MOMENTS?
YES!

DOES HE KNOW HOW TO TURN YOU INTO A DERANGED, INSECURE, SOBBING LUNATIC, INCAPABLE OF MAKING THE TEENSIEST MOVE WITHOUT QUESTIONING YOUR ENTIRE EXISTENCE ON EARTH?
YES.

THE GOOD ONES ARE ALWAYS JUST A LITTLE OVERQUALIFIED.

I HAVE TO MEET SOMEONE SOON, CATHY.
I KNOW WHAT YOU MEAN, CHARLENE.

IT ISN'T THE MOTHERHOOD URGE... IT ISN'T FEAR OF AGING...
I KNOW.

IT'S JUST SOMETHING ABOUT THIS COLD, SNOWY TIME OF YEAR... SOMETHING I DON'T THINK A MAN COULD EVEN UNDERSTAND....

IT'S THREE FULL MONTHS BEFORE HE'D EXPECT TO SEE YOU IN A BATHING SUIT.
I WANT HIM AND I WANT HIM **NOW!**

I CAN'T BUY THESE RELATIONSHIP BOOKS. THE SALESCLERK WILL THINK I'M HAVING PROBLEMS WITH MY BOYFRIEND.
WOMEN'S STUDIES
MEN'S STUDIES

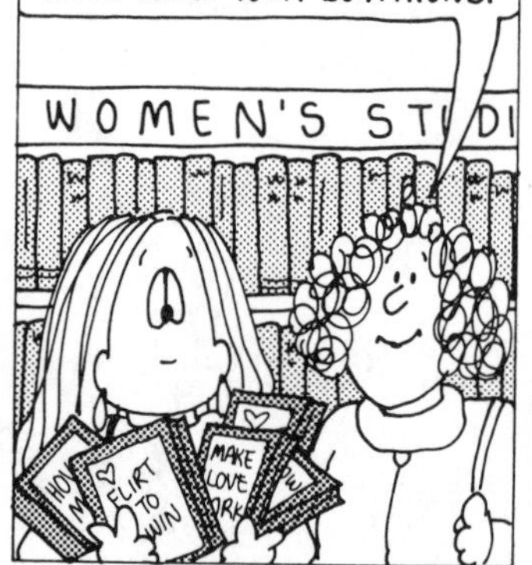
CATHY, EVERYONE YOU **KNOW** KNOWS YOU'RE HAVING PROBLEMS WITH YOUR BOYFRIEND.
FLIRT TO WIN
MAKE LOVE WORK

ALL **YOUR** FRIENDS KNOW. ALL **MY** FRIENDS KNOW. YOUR PARENTS KNOW. YOUR BOYFRIEND KNOWS.... WHAT DO YOU CARE IF SOME SALESCLERK YOU NEVER MET KNOWS??

IT'S HARD TO LOSE THE ONE PERSON LEFT IN THE WORLD WHO MIGHT THINK I'M DOING BRILLIANTLY.
FLIRT TO WIN
MAKE LOVE WORK

MAYBE YOU SHOULD KEEP ELECTRA IN THE KITCHEN TO HELP HOUSEBREAK HER, CATHY.
YES! I'LL TRY THAT!
START BEING MORE STERN.
THAT'S A GOOD IDEA!
OR CALL A TRAINER.
EXCELLENT SUGGESTION!

I DO NOT NEED YOUR OPINIONS, MOTHER! I KNOW WHAT I'M DOING! I HAVE EVERYTHING UNDER CONTROL!!

YOU MAY RULE HER HEART, BUT YOU WILL NEVER CONTROL HER BRAIN.
Guisewite

"CHAPTER ONE: LEARN TO BAT EYES..."
PUT THAT DOWN, CHARLENE. IF YOU WANT TO MEET SOMEONE, JUST DO WHAT MEN DO.

HI, I'M RICHARD! I'M SUCCESSFUL, OVER 30 AND READY TO SHARE MY LIFE WITH SOMEONE!
OH, RICHARD!

HI, I'M CHARLENE! I'M SUCCESSFUL, OVER 30 AND READY TO SHARE MY LIFE WITH SOMEONE!
AACK!

"CHAPTER ONE: LEARN TO BAT EYES..."
Guisewite

"HOW TO MESMERIZE A MAN FROM THE FIRST MOMENT HE SEES YOU.... USE YOUR WOMANLY CHARMS TO CREATE AN AURA OF INTRIGUE FROM WHICH HE'LL NEVER ESCAPE..."

THIS IS GOING TO CHANGE MY WHOLE RELATIONSHIP, CHARLENE!
CATHY, TIPS LIKE THAT WON'T WORK ON IRVING.

OF COURSE THEY WILL! I KNOW EXACTLY WHAT TO SAY TO HIM NOW!

PRETEND YOU HAVEN'T KNOWN ME FOR THE LAST EIGHT YEARS.

THERE'S NOTHING WRONG WITH GETTING A FEW POINTERS ON HOW TO FLIRT AND BE ENTICING TO A MAN, CATHY.

THINK ABOUT IT! IF YOU PUT THE SAME EFFORT INTO PERFECTING YOUR RELATIONSHIP SKILLS THAT YOU PUT INTO YOUR CAREER, LOOK AT WHAT YOU'D HAVE!!

MASS HYSTERIA, 7,000 SCRAPS OF PAPER AND A DEAD PLANT.

OK, FINE. LET'S NOT USE YOUR DESK AS AN EXAMPLE.

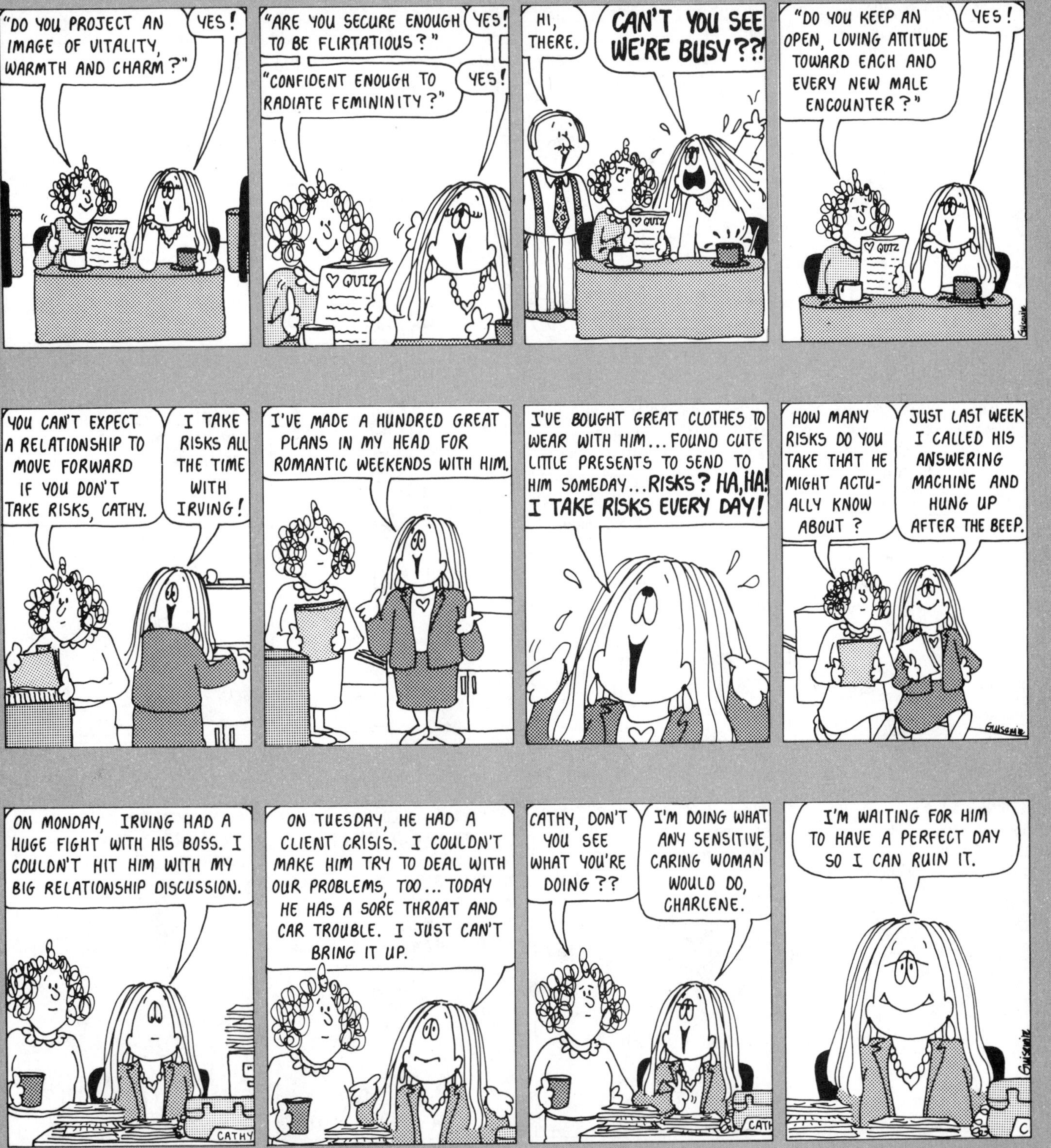

CATHY, DON'T YOU SEE WHAT YOU'RE DOING??
I'M DOING WHAT ANY SENSITIVE, CARING WOMAN WOULD DO, CHARLENE.

I'M WAITING FOR HIM TO HAVE A PERFECT DAY SO I CAN RUIN IT.

CHARLENE COACHED ME FOR TWO HOURS ON HAVING MY TALK WITH IRVING TONIGHT... IF I DON'T HAVE IT, I WON'T BE ABLE TO FACE HER...

...BUT SHE DOESN'T SEE HOW CUTE HE LOOKS RIGHT NOW... SHE DOESN'T KNOW HOW COZY EVERYTHING SEEMS TONIGHT...

CATHY?? WHY AREN'T YOU HAVING YOUR BIG TALK WITH IRVING?
FORGET IT, CHARLENE! JUST FORGET I EVER MET YOU!!

I DECIDED IT WOULD BE EASIER TO JUST BREAK UP WITH YOU.

"AN ANSWERING MACHINE PROGRAMMED WITH A CONFIDENT AND VIVACIOUS MESSAGE IS A GREAT WAY TO INSTILL THAT EXTRA BIT OF DESIRE IN A MAN."
The Art of Romance

"SOUND UNAVAILABLE AND UNATTAINABLE ON YOUR RECORDING, AND YOU UNLEASH THE FULL POWER OF A MAN'S IMAGINATION, DRIVING HIM WILD FOR A CHANCE TO SEE YOU AGAIN."
The Art of Roman

RING
YES!!

"TO ATTAIN BEST RESULTS, YOU MAY HAVE TO ACTUALLY LEAVE THE HOUSE NOW AND THEN...."
The Art of Romance

THINGS I SHOULD HAVE DONE AT WORK...
THINGS I WISH I'D SAID TO IRVING...
diet

THINGS I PROMISED MYSELF I'D NEVER DO AGAIN THAT I DID ANYWAY.
WAYS I MADE MYSELF MISERABLE THAT I COULD HAVE AVOIDED.
diet

THINGS I COULD HAVE DONE FOR MY FAMILY, MY PUPPY, MY FRIENDS, MY CO-WORKERS, MY NEIGHBORS, MY FINANCES, MY HOME, MY CLOSETS, MY DIET AND MILLIONS OF PEOPLE IN NEED WHOM I'VE NEVER MET.

EVEN WHEN I'M NOT GOING ANYWHERE, I HAVE 300 POUNDS OF LUGGAGE WITH ME.
diet

SOME CALL IT "THE NEW TRADITIONALISM." SOME CALL IT "RETROFEMINISM." SOME CALL IT A BAD JOKE.
HOW TO FLIRT
HOW TO FLIRT

WHATEVER THE LABEL, MANY WOMEN WHO POSTPONED MARRIAGE FOR CAREERS ARE NOW TRYING TO REDISCOVER THE DELICATE, FEMININE ART OF WOOING A MAN'S HEART.
HOW TO FLIRT
HOW TO FLIRT

CAN A GENERATION DEVOTED TO RAISING WOMEN'S SELF-ESTEEM REALLY REVERT TO HELPLESS GIGGLES AND DEMURE LITTLE BLUSHES? ONLY TIME WILL TELL.
HELLO. I WANT TO HAVE YOUR BABY.
HOW TO FLIRT

MEANWHILE, BOOK SALES ARE UP.
HOW TO FLIRT
HOW TO FLIRT

I TOLD MY MOTHER I DIDN'T CARE ABOUT EVER GETTING MARRIED, CATHY.
WE ALL TOLD OUR MOTHERS THAT.
HOW TO ATTRACT A MAN

WHAT WOULD MY MOTHER THINK IF SHE SAW ME ALL DECKED OUT, STUDYING A DATING MANUAL IN THE LADIES ROOM OF A SUSHI BAR?
YOUR MOTHER ISN'T HERE, CHARLENE.
HOW

YOUR MOTHER LIVES 2,000 MILES AWAY! IN A DIFFERENT TIME ZONE! SHE'S PROBABLY IN BED RIGHT NOW!!

COME ON... JUST PRETEND WE CAME FOR DINNER.
I FEEL MY MOTHER SMIRKING AT ME IN HER SLEEP!!!

I HAVE SOMEONE TO FIX YOU UP WITH, CHARLENE!
IS HE HANDSOME? IS HE SUCCESSFUL? IS HE FUNNY?

IRVING HAS A FRIEND WHOSE BROTHER KNOWS A WOMAN WHO WORKS WITH THE COUSIN OF SOMEONE WHO LIVES ACROSS THE STREET FROM A GUY WHO'S SUPPOSED TO BE CUTE.

THIS IS HUMILIATING! WHY DON'T I JUST WEAR A BIG SIGN AROUND MY NECK WITH MY PHONE NUMBER ON IT?!!
RIP!
RIP RIP!!

YOU ALREADY TRIED THAT LAST FALL.
DOES HE HAVE ANY HAIR LEFT ON HIS HEAD AT ALL?

JUST SAY YOU'LL MEET HIM FOR DINNER. HOW BAD COULD IT BE?
OH, NO. DINNER LASTS WAY TOO LONG FOR A BLIND DATE, CATHY.

MEET HIM FOR DRINKS.
NO. DRINKS COME BEFORE DINNER. TOO AWKWARD.
LUNCH.
LUNCH IS TOO BRIGHT. NO. NO DIRECT SUNLIGHT.

I'LL DRIVE PAST YOU AT THE INTERSECTION OF HARPER AND MAIN AT 6:15 P.M. PUT A RED CARNATION ON YOUR ANTENNA!

WHEW. WHAT A RISK-TAKER.
IT HAPPENS TO BE FOUR FULL BLOCKS OUT OF MY WAY.

THIS IS THE PERFECT BLIND DATE, CATHY. I'VE ARRANGED TO PASS HIM AT THE INTERSECTION AT EXACTLY 6:15. IF WE LIKE WHAT WE SEE, WE STOP THE CARS. IF NOT, WE JUST DRIVE OFF!

OUR TIME IS TOO PRECIOUS TO WASTE ON PHONY CHITCHAT WITH SOMEONE UNLESS THERE'S A TOTAL, MUTUAL ATTRACTION.

...WAIT! THAT'S HIM, CHARLENE! THAT'S THE CAR!
HIM?? BLEAH. I'M NOT STOPPING FOR HIM!!

HE JUST CRASHED A RED LIGHT.
COME BACK HERE! MY PERM ONLY LOOKS LIKE THIS THE FIRST WEEK!

LET'S JUST STAY IN TONIGHT, IRVING.
OK, BUT WHEN WE STAY IN YOU SAY WE NEVER GO OUT LIKE OTHER COUPLES.

YOU'RE RIGHT. LET'S GO OUT.
WHEN WE GO OUT YOU SAY WE NEVER STAY IN LIKE OTHER COUPLES.

LET'S GO OUT FOR A LITTLE BIT AND THEN COME HOME FOR A LITTLE BIT AND THEN, NO MATTER WHAT ALL THE OTHER COUPLES ARE DOING TONIGHT, WE'LL BE COVERED!
AAUGHH!

OR, ONE OF US COULD GO OUT AND ONE STAY IN, IN WHICH CASE WE'D ALSO BE COVERED...

Yap
Yap
Yap
ELECTRA, IT'S 3:00 IN THE MORNING... I CAN'T TAKE YOU OUT NOW.

Yap
Yap
Yap
IT'S DARK AND FREEZING OUT-SIDE. I'M TOO SLEEPY. I CAN'T GET UP.

YAP
YAP
YAP
LEAVE ME ALONE! JUST GO ON THE FLOOR! I'LL CLEAN IT UP TOMORROW!!

I DON'T THINK I'M READY TO BE A MOTHER.
Guisewite

EXCELLENT JOB, CATHY!
UH-OH.
Guisewite

YOUR PERFORMANCE HAS BEEN BRILLIANT!
ANY TIME YOU COMPLIMENT ME I KNOW YOU'RE ABOUT TO MAKE ME DO SOMETHING HORRIBLE, MR. PINKLEY.

YOU'RE SHARP! TENACIOUS! DILIGENT! DYNAMIC!!
IT MUST BE REALLY HIDEOUS! A HIDEOUS NIGHTMARE ASSIGNMENT!

AND HAVE I MENTIONED WHAT REMARKABLE INTUITION YOU HAVE??
AACK.

I KNOW YOU WON'T MAKE ME GO GROVELING TO A CLIENT THAT YOU INFURIATED, MR. PINKLEY.
I KNOW YOU WON'T LET ME DOWN WHEN I REALLY NEED YOU, CATHY.

I KNOW YOU WON'T HUMILIATE ME JUST TO SAVE YOUR OWN PRIDE!
I KNOW YOU WON'T FORGET ALL THE TIMES I'VE BEEN THERE FOR YOU!

AFTER EVERYTHING WE'VE BEEN THROUGH TOGETHER, I KNOW YOU WON'T DO THIS TO ME!!!

THE STAND-OFF IS OVER, BUT THE GUILT-OFF HAS JUST BEGUN.
CHARLENE
Guisewite

WHY CAN'T JAN GO ON THIS BUSINESS TRIP? I HAVE A NEW PUPPY TO TAKE CARE OF.
JAN HAS FOUR CHILDREN.
PINKLEY

WHY CAN'T RICK GO? I HAVE A CRISIS WITH MY BOYFRIEND I HAVE TO RESOLVE.
RICK'S IN THE MIDDLE OF A DIVORCE.
PINKLEY

WHY CAN'T BOB GO? I HAVE 10 OTHER CLIENT EMERGENCIES TO DEAL WITH!
BOB HAS SIX CHILDREN, A CRUMBLING MARRIAGE, THE STOMACH FLU AND IS HOLDING DOWN TWO JOBS.

I LOVE A COMPANY WITH A SENSE OF COMPETITION.
PINKLEY
Guisewite

I GUESS YOU'RE RIGHT, MOM. THANKS.
ENJOY YOUR BUSINESS TRIP, DEAR.

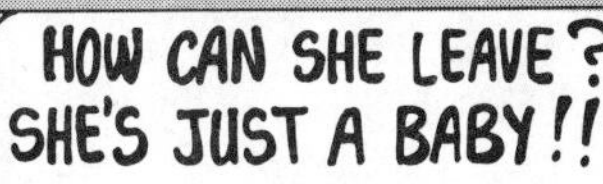

DUE TO TRAFFIC BACKUPS, YOUR FLIGHT WILL BE DE-LAYED ANOTHER TWO HOURS.
GATE 201

HOWEVER, WE REQUEST YOU STAY IN THE IMMEDIATE BOARDING AREA IN CASE WE CAN TAKE OFF SOONER.
GATE 201

IT WOULD DO YOU NO GOOD TO LEAVE ANYWAY, AS THE PAY PHONES ARE ALL BROKEN, THE WASHROOMS ARE ALL BEING CLEANED, THE GIFT SHOPS ARE ALL UNDER CONSTRUCTION, AND THE SNACK BARS ARE ALL BEING PICKETED.

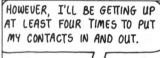

ON A BRIGHTER NOTE, THIS IS THE FIRST TIME IN HISTORY THE INTERCOM HAS WORKED.
GATE 201

I HATE BEING SQUASHED IN THE MIDDLE SEAT. WILL YOU TRADE WITH ME?
I COULD.

HOWEVER, I'LL BE GETTING UP AT LEAST FOUR TIMES TO PUT MY CONTACTS IN AND OUT.

I'LL GET UP TWICE TO FIX MY HAIR, THREE TIMES TO REDO MY MAKEUP, AND AT LEAST FIVE MORE TIMES BEFORE, DURING AND AFTER DINNER JUST ON GENERAL PRINCIPLE.

NEVER MIND.
NEVER UNDERESTI-MATE THE CLOUT OF TRAVELING WITH SIX LADIES' ROOMS.

I RESERVED A CAR TWO DAYS AGO. THE PAPER-WORK SHOULD BE ALL READY.
WE HAVE NO RECORD OF YOU.
CAR RENTAL

I SPECIFICALLY ASKED FOR A SUBCOMPACT.
ALL WE HAVE IS A FIVE-DOOR STATION WAGON.
CAR RENTAL

I WAS QUOTED $26 A DAY!!
$55 A DAY. STA-TION WAGON, AND IT'LL TAKE AN HOUR TO WRITE UP!
AR RENTAL

FINE. BUT I'M GOING TO GLARE AT YOU THE WHOLE TIME!!
IT'S ALMOST IMPOSSIBLE TO LOSE A CUSTOM-ER WHO'S GET-TING 500 BONUS POINTS.

I'M BETWEEN MEETINGS, MOM. I WANTED TO SEE IF ELECTRA'S OK.
PERFECT! I LEFT MY SHOES OUT ALL NIGHT AND SHE DIDN'T TOUCH THEM. HERE. I'LL PUT HER ON.

HI, ELECTRA! YOU DIDN'T EAT GRANDMA'S SHOES! WHAT A GOOD GIRL! WHAT A SMART BABY! TELL GRANDMA TO GIVE YOU A NICE BIG BONE!

MOTHERHOOD: FOR EVERY MOMENT OF PRIDE, AN HOUR OF EMBARRASSMENT.

YOU CAN'T FLY ALL THIS WAY AND NOT HAVE DESSERT, CATHY!
OH, NO. NO DESSERT, THANKS.

OUR CITY'S **FAMOUS** FOR DESSERTS!
I ALREADY HAD YOUR FAMOUS BREAKFAST BUFFET... FOUR-HOUR LUNCH...COCKTAIL HOUR AND FIVE-COURSE DINNER.

WE'RE **ALL** HAVING DESSERT!
YOU GO AHEAD. I'LL JUST RUN UP TO MY ROOM AND MAKE SOME CALLS SO I'LL BE READY FOR OUR MEETINGS TOMORROW.

HELLO, MOM? PLEASE FEDERAL EXPRESS MY BIGGER SKIRT.

"GET TRAVELER'S CHECKS INSTANTLY, 24 HOURS A DAY, AT ANY OF OUR 36,000 LOCATIONS."
SORRY. YOU HAVEN'T PRE-REGISTERED FOR YOUR P.I.N. NUMBER.
TRAVELERS CHECKS

"GET CASH INSTANTLY ON YOUR CHARGE CARD AT ANY OF OUR 75,000 LOCATIONS."
SORRY. THIS MACHINE IS TEMPORARILY OUT OF FUNDS.
CASH
TRAVEL CHECK

"GET CASH INSTANTLY WITH YOUR BANK ATM CARD AT 98,000 LOCATIONS WORLDWIDE."

SORRY. YOUR CARD ISN'T CODED FOR THIS MACHINE.

UNIVERSAL ATM

I HAD TO GET A 6 A.M. FLIGHT, SKIP BREAKFAST AND PAY $45 FOR A CAB.... BUT IT'S WORTH IT TO GET BACK TO MY LITTLE PUPPY SOONER...
AXI

I WOULD HAVE CRAWLED ON MY HANDS AND KNEES TO SEE MY PRECIOUS BABY!! MY ELECTRA! I'M HOME! LEAP INTO MY ARMS!! MOMMY IS HOME!

CHOMP
CHOMP
CHOMP
PUPPY TREATS

THINK BACK TO THE DAYS WHEN YOU HAD TO FINISH WATCHING "BULLWINKLE" RE-RUNS BEFORE YOU'D SAY HELLO TO YOUR MOTHER.
CHOMP
CHOMP
CHOMP
CHOMP
PUPPY TREATS

IF YOU BRUSH ELECTRA'S HAIR FOR TWO MINUTES EACH MORNING, SHE'LL BE EASIER TO GROOM HER WHOLE LIFE.
I KNOW, MOM.

IF YOU SAY ONE FIRM "NO," IT WILL BE 10 TIMES MORE EFFECTIVE THAN 10 TENTATIVE "NOs."
I KNOW, MOM.

IF YOU TAKE ELECTRA OUT AT EXACTLY THE SAME TIME EACH...
I KNOW, MOM!! ENOUGH!! I'VE HEARD ENOUGH!!

HOW MANY MOTHERS CAN TURN JUST A FEW PEARLS OF WISDOM INTO A CHOKER?
ELECTRA

ELECTRA WAS PERFECT WHILE I WAS GONE, MOM??
OF COURSE SHE WAS PERFECT!
ELECTRA

SHE...UM... DIDN'T HAVE ANY ACCI-DENTS??
CERTAINLY NOT. SET CLEAR RULES FOR YOUNG ONES, AND THEY WILL ALWAYS FOLLOW THEM!

WHEN YOU'VE BEEN A PARENT AS LONG AS I HAVE, YOU'LL KNOW THE IMPORTANCE OF ESTABLISHING WHO'S BOSS!!

NOW MAY I CALL THE CARPET FU-MIGATOR??
GIVE HER A SECOND TO BACK OUT OF THE DRIVEWAY.

ELECTRA, I'M PUTTING THIS NEWSPAPER ON THE FLOOR IN CASE I CAN'T COME HOME AT LUNCH TO TAKE YOU OUT.
CATHY, DO YOU ACTU-ALLY THINK SHE UNDERSTANDS WHY YOU PUT NEWSPAPER ON THE FLOOR ??
SHE'S VERY SMART, IRVING.

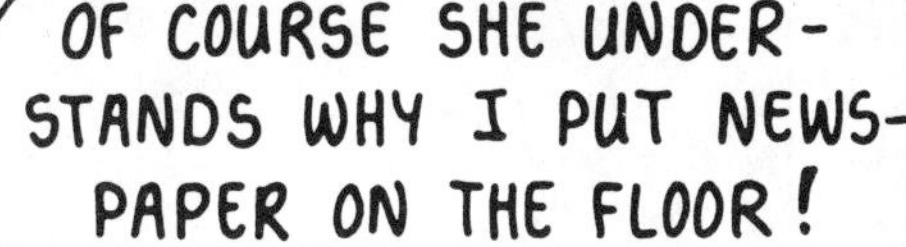
OF COURSE SHE UNDER-STANDS WHY I PUT NEWS-PAPER ON THE FLOOR!

SO I CAN READ SNOOPY.
Guisewite

YOU'RE GOING HOME ON TIME FOR ONCE, CATHY ?
I HAVE TO GET OUT OF HERE, CHARLENE.
CHARLENE

ALL I'VE DONE FOR TWO WEEKS IS WORK... BUSINESS TRIPS... BUSINESS MEALS... DEADLINES... REPORTS... POWER BATTLES... EMERGENCIES...
CHARLENE

FOR ONCE I HAVE TO JUST GO HOME AND GET BACK IN TOUCH WITH MY GENTLE, FEMININE SIDE...

.... THE HOUSE CLEANER.

HOW ARE YOU DOING, CATHY ?
OH, IRVING, MY PLANE TRIP TO MY MEETING WAS A NIGHTMARE !!

THAT WAS FIVE DAYS AGO. YOU MADE IT.
THE FIRST DAY OF MEETINGS WAS HORRIBLE !

THAT'S ALL OVER NOW. IT'S HISTORY. HOW ARE YOU TODAY ?
FINE. TODAY I'M JUST FINE.

SOMETIMES I FEEL LIKE A NEWSPAPER THAT GOT THROWN OUT BEFORE ANYONE READ IT.

IRVING, I WANT US TO LEARN TO LISTEN TO EACH OTHER BETTER.
OK.

LISTENING IS AN ART... LISTENING CAN BE HARD WORK... ... BUT THE GREAT COUPLES OF THE WORLD ARE THE COUPLES WHO REALLY KNOW HOW TO LISTEN TO ONE ANOTHER !!

OK.

ONE OF US HAS TO SAY SOMETHING.
ALWAYS A CATCH...

THE WINTER COATS ARE PUT AWAY...

THE HEAVY WOOLS ARE CAST ASIDE...

THE DYNAMIC WOMAN BURSTS INTO APRIL WITH A LOOK, A FLAIR, A FEELING ALL HER OWN...

I HAVEN'T HAD TIME TO GO SHOPPING YET.

AFTER TWO YEARS OF BLEAK SALES, THE FASHION INDUSTRY PRESENTS A WHOLE NEW CONCEPT IN DRESSING! THE WRAP!
E WRAP!

SEE? WRAP IT AROUND YOUR MIDDLE, AND IT'S A SKIRT... WRAP IT AROUND YOUR LEGS, IT'S PANTS... WRAP IT AROUND YOUR TOP, IT'S A TOP...
THE WRAP!

IT'S OUR LITTLE WAY OF SAYING, **IF YOU DON'T LIKE WHAT WE CREATE, HERE'S THE FABRIC, GO MAKE YOUR OWN STUPID CLOTHES!**
AP!

...HELLO, BUYING OFFICE? BRACE YOURSELF FOR ANOTHER RECORD-BREAKING SEASON.
WRAP!

ONE OF OUR FASHION "MUSTS" FOR SPRING COMES FROM THE MEN'S WORLD: THE VEST!
I THOUGHT WE DIDN'T WANT TO DRESS LIKE MEN.
NEW

WE DON'T. MEN BUY ONE BORING VEST AND WEAR IT THEIR WHOLE LIVES.

WOMEN'S VESTS COME IN WILD PRINTS AND BROCADES, GUARANTEEING THAT YOU NOT ONLY NEED TO BUY **ONE PER OUTFIT**, BUT THEY'LL **ALL** LOOK RIDICULOUS BY THE FOURTH OF JULY!!

IN THE WORLD OF FASHION, WOMEN ALWAYS MAINTAIN OUR OWN STYLE.
BANKRUPTCY.
NEW

I CAN SEE RIGHT THROUGH THIS DRESS.
IT'S OUR SEXIEST SPRING LOOK...THE LUSCIOUS CURVES OF THE FEMALE FORM UNDER A LAYER OF WISPY CHIFFON!

REALLY? MY BOY-FRIEND WOULD LIKE THIS??
LIKE?? YOU'LL TANTALIZE HIM! YOU'LL BEGUILE HIM! YOU'LL HAVE HIM UNDER YOUR SPELL!!

....HI, HANDSOME...
CATHY, I CAN SEE RIGHT THROUGH THAT DRESS!

I WANT MY MONEY BACK, PLUS $50 IN HUMILIATION COMPENSATION.
Mall
Guisewite

OH, THAT LOOKS DARLING ON YOU, CATHY. YOU SHOULD GET IT!
MOM, IT MAKES ME LOOK LIKE A MEAT LOAF.

YOU LOOK JUST BEAUTIFUL IN THAT! YOU SHOULD GET IT!
I LOOK LIKE BOZO THE CLOWN.

YOU LOOK SO STUNNING! YOU LOOK LIKE A MOVIE STAR!
MOTHER, YOU'RE SUPPOSED TO BE HELPING!!

IT'S ALMOST IMPOSSIBLE TO REJECT SOMETHING WHEN IT HAS MY DAUGHTER IN IT.
Guisewite

WE HAVE SOME LOVELY NEW BUSINESS CLOTHES...
NO. I SPEND MY WHOLE LIFE AT THE OFFICE. I'M TIRED OF BUYING BUSINESS CLOTHES.

WE HAVE CUTE NEW KICKING-AROUND CLOTHES.
NO. THE ONLY TIME I'M NOT AT WORK, I'M RUNNING ERRANDS. I'M TIRED OF BUYING "KICKING-AROUND" CLOTHES.

I WANT FUN CLOTHES! FRIVOLOUS CLOTHES! SEXY, CAREFREE, EXOTIC, PASSIONATE CLOTHES!!

I WANT CLOTHES FOR THE PART OF MY LIFE I WILL NEVER ACTUALLY HAVE TIME TO EXPERIENCE.
Guisewite

IT TOOK ME THREE BOXES OF FROZEN GIRL SCOUT COOKIES TO GET THROUGH THE FIRST BOX OF TAX RECEIPTS...
ICE
ICE CREAM

TWO CHOCOLATE ÉCLAIRS TO WADE THROUGH THE CANCELED CHECKS... AND FOUR "SINGLE SERVING" PIZZAS TO FIND THE PHONE NUMBER OF MY ACCOUNTANT....

OH, ELECTRA, I'M A HOPELESS, DISORGANIZED, PATHETIC WRECK! HOW CAN YOU STILL LOOK AT ME WITH SUCH A SWEET, LOVING FACE??

THE WORSE THINGS GET, THE BETTER WE EAT.

WASHINGTON SOURCES HAVE ANNOUNCED THAT, IN THE EVENT OF A NUCLEAR ATTACK, IRS AGENTS ARE EXPECTED TO RESUME COLLECTING TAXES WITHIN 30 DAYS.

NO ONE KNOWS HOW AN AGENCY THAT STILL CAN'T GET ITS "QUESTION HOTLINE" TO WORK HAS BEEN ABLE TO CREATE A PLAN FOR COLLECTING YOUR TAXES AFTER YOUR CITY'S BEEN NUKED...

...HOWEVER, ONE THING REMAINS FAIRLY CLEAR....

CROSS "HAD A STOMACHACHE" OFF MY LIST OF EXCUSES FOR NOT FILING THIS YEAR.

I MADE $12,216 IN HOUSE PAYMENTS LAST YEAR, AND REDUCED THE AMOUNT I OWE BY $1,300.

I MADE $3,241 IN CAR PAYMENTS, AND STILL OWE $6,700 ON A CAR THAT RUNS ONLY TWO DAYS A WEEK.

I WORKED HARDER THAN I'VE EVER WORKED IN MY LIFE, WAS MORE CAREFUL ABOUT WHAT I SPENT, AND ENDED THE YEAR $85,400 IN THE HOLE.

AS LONG AS I'M SINKING INTO THE MUCK, I MIGHT AS WELL BE WEARING A NICE NEW PAIR OF SHOES.
SHOES

I CAN'T STAND PAYING TAXES IF I THINK THE GOVERNMENT ISN'T USING MY MONEY CAREFULLY.
REST ASSURED, CATHY...
ACCOUNTANT

ALL THE MONEY YOU SWEATED AND SLAVED FOR THIS YEAR WENT TO HELP FINANCE THE IRS' $1.9 MILLION STUDY OF HOW LONG IT TAKES PEOPLE TO FILL OUT TAX FORMS.

IN FACT, **ALL THE MONEY YOU WILL EVER MAKE IN YOUR LIFE** WILL GO TOWARD PAYING OFF THE RESEARCH TEAM WHO SPENT FIVE YEARS DETERMINING THAT IT WILL TAKE YOU 24 MINUTES TO READ THE INSTRUCTIONS ON FORM 1040 EZ!

...EXCEPT, OF COURSE, THE $150 YOU'LL BE PAYING ME TO **EXPLAIN** THE INSTRUCTIONS.
ACCOUNTANT

DO YOU REALIZE WHAT A TAX BREAK YOU'D GET IF YOU WERE MARRIED, CATHY?
THAT ISN'T TRUE ANYMORE, MOM.
Misc. Recpts.

OF COURSE IT IS! IF YOU WERE MARRIED...
FINE. SAY I GOT MARRIED. **THEN** WOULD YOU STOP?! THEN COULD WE NOT HAVE THIS CONVERSATION EVERY YEAR?!

THEN COULD WE TALK ABOUT SOMETHING ELSE FOR ONCE??!

DO YOU REALIZE WHAT A TAX BREAK YOU'D GET IF YOU HAD CHILDREN?
Misc. Recpts.

JAN. 19, 1988:

ORDERED $49 OF TAKEOUT FOOD BECAUSE I DIDN'T WANT THE CASHIER TO THINK I WAS EATING DINNER ALONE.

1988 EXPENSES

MAY 3, 1988:
SPENT $76 ON GOURMET DESSERTS FOR A DINNER PARTY. ATE THEM MYSELF BEFORE THE GUESTS ARRIVED.
1988 EXPENSES

AUG. 26, 1988:
ATE $103 OF FROZEN FOOD BECAUSE THE POWER WENT OFF FOR 10 MINUTES AND I DIDN'T WANT IT ALL TO MELT AND GO TO WASTE.

THEY TOLD ME TO BUILD A NEST EGG, BUT NO ONE MENTIONED I WASN'T SUPPOSED TO EAT IT.

FOUR POUNDS?? I LOST FOUR POUNDS!!

ELECTRA, I LOST FOUR POUNDS! OH, I'M SO HAP-PY! LIFE IS SO WONDER-FUL! YOU'RE WONDERFUL!

WHAT A BEAUTIFUL PUPPY!! I LOVE MY BEAUTIFUL PUP-PY! LET'S FIND YOU A TOY! LET'S FIX YOU A SNACK! LIFE IS GRAND!! I LOST FOUR POUNDS!!

ATTENTION, DOGS OF THE WORLD: TO IMPROVE YOUR QUALITY OF LIFE, PUT YOUR NOSE ON THE DIAL OF THE SCALE AND SHOVE TO THE RIGHT ONE INCH.
Guisewite

MY TAXES ARE PAID, AND MY NEW FINANCIAL ORGANIZER IS IN MY PURSE.
U.S. MAIL

FROM THIS MOMENT ON, EVERY DIME WILL BE RECORDED, EVERY TRANSACTION DOCUMENTED, EVERY RECEIPT NOTARIZED, INDEXED AND FILED!

U.S. MAIL

THE ONE DAY OF THE YEAR I'M FULLY PREPARED TO KEEP TRACK OF MY MONEY, I HAVE NOTHING LEFT TO SPEND.
U.S. MAIL

YES, UM... I'M MEETING A MR. FILPOT FOR DINNER.
CHECK IN THE BAR. MAYBE HE'S WAITING THERE.

AHEM... ACTUALLY, MAYBE YOU COULD JUST SEAT ME AND SHOW HIM TO THE TABLE IF HE'S HERE.
AH, YES. OF COURSE. I UNDERSTAND.

I WILL BRING MR. FILPOT TO YOUR TABLE WITH THE UTMOST OF DISCRETION.
THANK YOU. THANK YOU SO MUCH.

WOULD YOU LIKE SOMETHING TO DRINK UNTIL YOUR **BLIND DATE** SHOWS UP??

PLEASE LET THAT BE HIM! FOR ONCE IN MY LIFE, LET ME HAVE A BLIND DATE WHO LOOKS LIKE THAT!

PLEASE... I WILL NEVER EAT ANOTHER FATTENING THING! I WILL NEVER SKIP ANOTHER WORKOUT! **OH, PLEASE, PLEASE PLEASE PLEASE...**

SORRY I'M LATE. THE XJS STALLED OUT WHILE I WAS **FAXING A 40G DEAL** TO THE **COAST**, AND THEN THE AUTO SERVICE WOULDN'T TAKE MY **PLATINUM** AMEX CARD!

I'LL HAVE THE BEEF STROGANOFF AND A BASKET OF GARLIC BREAD.
MIND IF I CHECK MY MACHINE? HA, HA! MY BEEPER'S ON THE BLINK!

YAK YAK MY BEEMER MY BOAT YAK YAK YAK...
THE SECOND THIS BLIND DATE IS OVER, I'M GOING TO GO MURDER CHARLENE.

YAK YAK YAK MY JACUZZI MY CLUB YAK YAK MY MASSEUSE...
I'LL GO TO HER HOME AND STRANGLE HER SCRAWNY NECK FOR FIXING ME UP WITH THIS GEEK.

MY CONDO YAK YAK YAK YAK YAK YAK MY BROKER YAK YAK
I'LL GO TO PRISON. SO WHAT? HAH! I'LL SPEND THE REST OF MY LIFE ROTTING BEHIND BARS, BUT I'LL HAVE MY REVENGE!!

....SO, WHAT ARE YOUR PLANS FOR THE FUTURE, CATHY?
GUISEWITE

WE HAVE NOTHING IN COMMON, BRADLEY.
I DIDN'T THINK IT WAS SO BAD FOR A FIRST DATE.
BISTRO
VALET PARK

WELL, NO. IT WASN'T HIDEOUS. IT'S JUST...
YOU HAVE TO GIVE THESE THINGS TIME!
BISTRO
VALET PARK

NO, REALLY. I CAN TELL. WE HAVE NO FUTURE. IT'S OVER. DONE. GOODBYE.
WE'LL TALK ABOUT IT OVER DINNER TOMORROW. EIGHTISH??
BISTRO
GUISEWITE

HOW CAN I BE SO GOOD AT DESTROYING THE RELATIONSHIPS I WANT, AND SO BAD AT GETTING OUT OF THE ONES I'M REPULSED BY?

CHARLENE, HOW COULD YOU FIX ME UP WITH...
YOU CAN'T YELL AT ME, CATHY. IT'S SECRETARIES WEEK!

FOR FIVE FULL DAYS, THE SECRETARIES OF THE WORLD ARE TO BE TREATED AS GODDESSES!

PAMPER US! COMPLIMENT US! WORSHIP US! SHOWER US WITH GIFTS!!

...AND REMIND US TO GET THE MEMO ON THIS OUT EARLIER NEXT YEAR....
ASAP
GUISEWITE

...AND ESPECI- ALLY FOR THE PRIDE AND CAMARADERIE YOU INSPIRE IN ALL THOSE AROUND YOU!

OH, MR. PINKLEY! THAT'S BEAUTIFUL!!

ATTENTION ALL EMPLOYEES: I KNOW YOU'RE ALL MUCH TOO BUSY TO SHOP FOR MY SECRETARIES WEEK GIFT, SO I'M RAISING MONEY TO BUY MY OWN LITTLE PRESENT.
CHARLENE

WHAT AM I BID FOR THE PHOTO NEGATIVES OF MR. PINKLEY AT THE OFFICE CHRISTMAS PARTY?... THE TRANSCRIPT OF CATHY'S LAST PERSONAL CALL TO IRVING?... CONFIDENTIAL SALARY INFORMATION ON THE MANAGEMENT SQUAD?...

...MY SECRET VIDEO, ENTITLED "AFFAIRS IN THE COPIER ROOM", VOLUMES I, II, III, AND....

IT'S INCREDIBLE HOW THEY ALL RALLY WHEN IT'S FOR A PROJECT THEY BELIEVE IN.
Guisewite

I WANT TO CALL THIS WOMAN BACK, BUT IT'S BEEN SO LONG SINCE WE'VE TALKED...
IN
IN
IN
CATHY

I'LL HAVE TO REHASH EVERYTHING I'VE BEEN DOING FOR THE LAST SIX MONTHS... I'LL HAVE TO LISTEN TO WHAT SHE'S BEEN DOING FOR THE LAST SIX MONTHS... WHERE WE'VE BEEN... WHO WE'VE SEEN... HOW WE'VE FELT....WHY WE HAVEN'T CALLED....
IN

TECHNOLOGY COMES FULL CIRCLE.

I COULD SAVE THREE HOURS BY WRITING HER A LETTER.
IN
IN
IN
CATHY
Guisewite

ARE YOU SURE YOU CAN CANCEL YOUR PLANS WITH ANDREA, CATHY?
SURE, IRVING. IT'S THE FIRST RULE OF WOMANHOOD: IF A MAN CALLS, THE WOMAN FRIEND IS DUMPED!
HELLO, ANDREA?
OH, CATHY! IT TOOK ALL DAY, BUT I HAVE A SITTER LINED UP FOR 7 TO 7:45, AND ANOTHER STARTING AT 7:30...
MY HUSBAND SHOULD BE HOME AT 9, UNLESS HE'S RUNNING LATE, IN WHICH CASE I HAVE A BACK-UP ON CALL FROM 9 TO 10:30... ...WHEW! I CAN'T WAIT TO GET OUT OF HERE!

THE SECOND RULE OF WOMANHOOD: A FRIEND CAN BE DUMPED, BUT A MOTHER IS FOREVER.
Guisewite

ZENITH WANTS A SNACK, CATHY. WHERE ARE YOUR CHEERIOS?
I DON'T HAVE ANY CHEERIOS, ANDREA.
DOG FOOD

OH, HA, HA! ALL MY REGULAR FRIENDS ARE MOTHERS! I FORGOT THERE WERE HOMES WITH NO CHEERIOS!!
WELL, EXCUSE ME.

OH, CATHY, I'M SORRY. I JUST FORGOT WHAT A SINGLE PERSON'S KITCHEN IS LIKE.
THAT'S OK, ANDREA. I WAS A LITTLE DEFENSIVE.

WHERE ARE YOUR ORGANIC RICE CAKES?
HERE. LET HER GNAW ON A FROZEN SINGLE-SERVING POUCH.
Guisewite

I THOUGHT YOU WERE TEACHING ELECTRA NOT TO JUMP, CATHY.
I AM. SHE'S NOT ALLOWED TO JUMP IF I'M WEARING A DRESS, SUIT OR NATURAL-FIBER SKIRT.

ALL DARK PANTS ARE "NO JUMPING" EXCEPT MY TWO OLDEST BLUE JEANS, UNLESS I'M WEARING THEM WITH MY SUEDE BOOTS, WHICH COULD BE SCRATCHED.

SHE CAN JUMP ON THE PINK COTTON SWEATER, THE TAN PULL-OVER, AND ANY OF THE SWEAT-SHIRTS EXCEPT, OF COURSE, THE LAVENDER "TON-SUR-TON"!

WHEN PEOPLE WONDER WHAT DOGS THINK ABOUT ALL DAY, THEY FORGET HOW MUCH MEMORIZATION IS INVOLVED.
Guisewite

AACK! ZENITH! THAT'S DOG FOOD! YOU DO NOT EAT DOG FOOD!!
CHOMP
CHOMP
DOG

YOU ARE NOT A DOG! YOU'RE A LITTLE PERSON! A LITTLE BILINGUAL, MUSICALLY GIFTED, 143 IQ PERSON!

WHY DO YOU THINK MOMMY HAS SPENT 24 HOURS A DAY ENRICHING YOUR INCREDIBLE LITTLE MIND WITH THE WHOLE DAZZLING SCOPE OF HUMAN POTENTIAL???

SHE SEEMS TO HAVE MASTERED BELLIGERENCE.
WHERE ARE YOUR BIODE-GRADABLE FACE WIPES?
SPLAT!
CHOMP CHOMP

ZENITH DEMANDS ATTENTION EVERY SECOND OF THE DAY, CATHY.
MY JOB IS LIKE THAT, TOO. A CRI-SIS EVERY SECOND!

SHE NEEDS THIS... WANTS THAT... SHE FUSSES, WHINES, SHRIEKS...
HA, HA! MY JOB IS EX-ACTLY LIKE THAT!

OH, PLEASE...THERE'S A BIG DIFFERENCE BETWEEN A LITTLE HUMAN BEING AND SOME JOB!

MINE IS NEVER GOING TO GROW UP!!

WHEN YOU SPEND TIME WITH YOUR MARRIED GIRLFRIENDS, YOU GET FIRED UP AND START NAGGING ME ABOUT MAKING A COMMITMENT, CATHY...

WHEN YOU SPEND TIME WITH YOUR SINGLE GIRLFRIENDS, YOU GET FIRED UP AND TRY TO TRICK ME INTO MAKING A COMMITMENT...

ANY TIME YOU GO OUT WITH THE GIRLS, I WIND UP GET-TING SOME SPEECH ABOUT COMMITMENT!
THEREFORE, IF YOU WERE WITH ME MORE OF THE TIME, WE WOULDN'T HAVE THESE PROBLEMS, WOULD WE?

AAUGH!!
SORRY. I JUST GOT OFF THE PHONE WITH MY MOTHER.

HI, SWEETIE. ARE YOU STILL PLANNING ON LUNCH THIS SUNDAY?

OF COURSE I'M PLANNING ON LUNCH, MOM!

IF YOU'RE TOO BUSY, I UNDERSTAND.

I'M NOT TOO BUSY.

WE COULD DO IT ANOTHER DAY IF YOU'RE BUSY.

I'M **NOT** BUSY.

WE COULD TALK ABOUT IT LATER IF YOU'RE BUSY RIGHT NOW.

I AM NOT BUSY NOW.

WE COULD JUST SKIP IT.

HOW WAS YOUR MOTHER'S DAY LUNCH, CATHY ?
GREAT UNTIL MOM WHIPPED OUT HER VIDEO OF FLO NEKERVIS' GRANDCHILDREN.

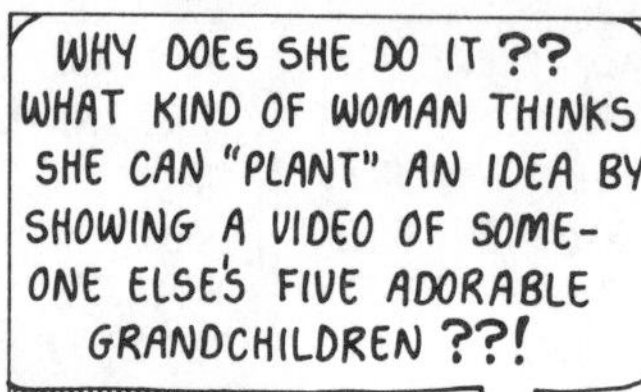

WHY DOES SHE DO IT ?? WHAT KIND OF WOMAN THINKS SHE CAN "PLANT" AN IDEA BY SHOWING A VIDEO OF SOMEONE ELSE'S FIVE ADORABLE GRANDCHILDREN ??!

...JUST WATCH A COUPLE MINUTES OF IT IRVING. AHEM... ...I JUST WANT YOU TO SEE WHAT I HAVE TO PUT UP WITH.

INCREDIBLE NEW DRESS, BUT I DIDN'T FIND SHOES TO GO WITH IT YET...

PERFECT SHOES, BUT NO MATCHING SKIRT... WONDERFUL SKIRT, BUT NO MATCHING BLOUSE... GREAT BLOUSE, BUT NO MATCHING PANTS...

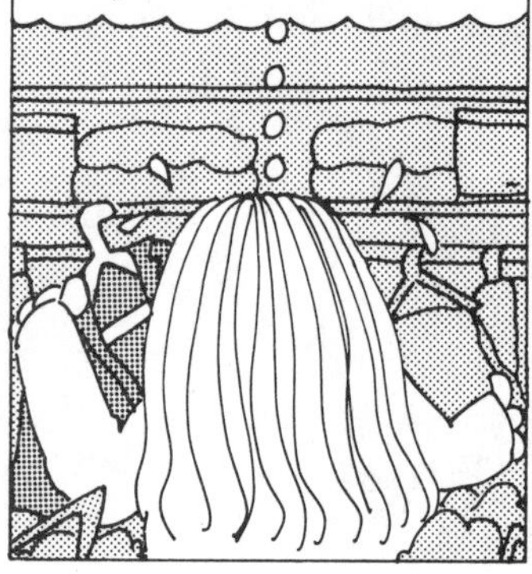

FABULOUS JACKET, BUT NO MATCHING SKIRT, PANTS, DRESS SHOES, JEWELRY OR BELT....

THE INDIVIDUAL PARTS OF ME ARE ALL PREPARED TO COME TO WORK, MR. PINKLEY, BUT AS A GROUP WE WON'T BE ABLE TO MAKE IT.

I SAID I DIDN'T WANT DESSERT, IRVING.
JUST HAVE A TASTE AND LEAVE THE REST, CATHY.

IF I HAVE A TASTE, I'LL FINISH THE WHOLE THING.
THAT'S RIDICULOUS! SEE? I'M JUST HAVING A TASTE!

IF I CAN HAVE A TASTE AND LEAVE THE REST, WHY CAN'T YOU HAVE A TASTE AND LEAVE THE REST ??!

MEN DATE. WOMEN HAVE RELATIONSHIPS.

ISOMETRIC EXERCISES TO DO IN THE CAR SO I DON'T GET ANTSY AND EAT MY LUNCH ON THE WAY TO WORK...
ISOMETRICS

MOTIVATIONAL TAPES SO I DON'T GET BORED AND EAT MY LUNCH ON THE WAY TO WORK...

SOOTHING ENVIRONMENTAL TAPES AND STEAMY LOVE STORY TAPES SO I DON'T GET ANNOYED AND EAT MY LUNCH ON THE WAY TO WORK...

DID YOU BRING YOUR LUNCH TODAY, CATHY ?
DIDN'T EVEN MAKE IT OUT OF THE DRIVEWAY.
CHARLENE

WHY DIDN'T YOU CANCEL THE GRIMES MEETING ?? WE'LL NEVER BE READY !
IF YOU WAIT IT OUT, SOMETIMES THE OTHER PERSON CANCELS AND THEN WE CAN BLAME ALL DELAYS ON HIM.

HE'LL BE HERE IN 20 MINUTES!
HE STILL COULD CANCEL! HE STILL MIGHT CANCEL!

GRIMES JUST CALLED AND CANCELED UNTIL NEXT WEEK.
YES! HA, HA! IT WORKED! WE'RE SAVED!!

A REPRIEVE! BREAK OUT THE CHAMPAGNE!! WE DID IT! HA, HA!
THIS OFFICE CELEBRATES CANCELLATIONS THE WAY SOME OFFICES CELEBRATE NEW BUSINESS.

IF I GET INVITED TO A MOONLIGHT BARBECUE IN JUNE, THIS WOULD BE PERFECT...

IF THE HANDSOME MAN I MEET AT THE BARBECUE TAKES ME DANCING EVERY NIGHT AND I LOSE 15 POUNDS BY THE FOURTH OF JULY, THIS WOULD BE ADORABLE...

IF WE SPEND AUGUST HORSEBACK RIDING IN THE FRENCH COUNTRYSIDE AND STOP FOR ESPRESSO AT A LITTLE CAFÉ, THIS WOULD BE DARLING TO TOSS OVER MY SHOULDERS AS THE SUN SETS AND THE MEDITERRANEAN BREEZE COOLS THE SULTRY RIVIERA AIR...

THIS WOULD BE CUTE TO WEAR TO THE GROCERY STORE.
GET REAL, MOM.

YAWN... ANOTHER HOUR UNTIL MY BREAK... I'M BORED TO DEATH...
ME, TOO... ..YAWN... WHERE'D YOU PUT THAT LAST CUSTOMER?
1
SWIMWEAR

ROOM #1... SHE'S PROBABLY JUST STUFFING HERSELF INTO THE FIRST BATHING SUIT...
HO, HUM... ...SHE COULD BE IN THERE ALL DAY...
CLICK!

AAACK!!
1
RIP
RIP
WAD
RIP

NOTHING LIGHTS UP A ROOM LIKE A NICE NEW FLUORESCENT BULB.
Guisewite

IF YOUR CHEST IS A LITTLE SMALL, THIS SWIMSUIT WILL SQUASH IT COMPLETELY FLAT...

IF YOUR STOMACH'S TOO BIG, THIS WILL SPREAD OUT LIKE GIANT NEON ARROWS POINTING AT THE FLAB... THIGHS TOO PLUMP? THIS ONE SQUISHES THEM INTO TWO BIG BULGES, ABOVE AND BELOW THE LEG LINE.

NO MATTER WHAT YOUR FIGURE PROBLEM, WE HAVE A SUIT THAT WILL MAKE IT WORSE!

YOU'RE TRYING THEM ON??
CURIOSITY TAKES OVER WHERE HOPE LEAVES OFF.
Guisewite

DO YOU WANT A LARGER SIZE?
NO. I DO NOT WANT A LARGER SIZE.

I AM SICK OF HAVING TO BUY BATHING SUITS TWO SIZES BIGGER THAN THE SIZE I WEAR IN ALL OTHER CLOTHES!

I AM NOT GOING UP TWO SIZES JUST BECAUSE THESE SPANDEX TUBES WERE STITCHED TOGETHER BY SOMEONE WHO HAS NEVER SEEN A HUMAN BODY! HAH! TELL THAT TO YOUR SALES MANAGER!!

NO NEED. OUR DRESSING ROOM MONITORS HAVE THE WHOLE THING ON VIDEOTAPE.
Guisewite

ELECTRA, YOU'RE SUPPOSED TO BE MY GUARD DOG. WHEN SOMEONE COMES TO THE DOOR, YOU'RE SUPPOSED TO BARK.

YOUR JOB IS TO PROTECT ME, OK. ANY TIME YOU HEAR A NOISE, BARK.

DING DONG!
AACK.

I DIDN'T HEAR ANY BARKING.
SHE SENSED THAT YOU WERE FRIENDLY.

HOW ABOUT THIS ONE WITH THE NICE RUFFLED SKIRT?
NO. A RUFFLED SKIRT MEANS YOU'RE TRYING TO HIDE YOUR REAR.

YOU **ARE** TRYING TO HIDE YOUR REAR.
I WANT A SUIT THAT HIDES MY REAR WITHOUT ANNOUNCING TO THE WORLD THAT I'M HIDING MY REAR!

FOR ONCE IN MY LIFE, I WANT A BATHING SUIT THAT DOESN'T RELY ON SOME OBVIOUS GIMMICK!

HOW ABOUT THIS ONE WITH THE GATHERED TOP THAT GIVES THE ILLUSION OF A BUSTLINE?
OK.

CAN YOU BEND OVER IN THE BATHING SUIT WITHOUT REVEALING ANYTHING YOU DON'T WANT REVEALED?
YES!

CAN YOU SIT AND THEN STAND UP WITHOUT HAVING TO TUG AT FIVE DIFFERENT AREAS OF THE SUIT?
YES!

CAN YOU LOOK AT THE BACK OF THE SUIT WITHOUT...
THUNK!

STRANGE HOW LIFE'S BIGGEST OBSTACLES ALWAYS SNEAK UP FROM BEHIND.

IF MEN HAD TO GO THROUGH A FRACTION OF WHAT WOMEN DO TO BUY A BATHING SUIT, THE POOLS AND BEACHES OF THE WORLD WOULD SHUT DOWN COMPLETELY!!

THAT'S NOT TRUE, CATHY. MEN HAVE THE SAME TROUBLE.
YOU DO??
WE HATE SEEING OURSELVES IN SWIMSUITS AFTER BEING INSIDE ALL WINTER.
REALLY??

IT'S EXACTLY THE SAME HORRIBLE PROBLEM FOR MEN AS IT IS FOR WOMEN.
OH, IRVING, YOU MAKE ME FEEL SO MUCH BETTER....

...SO AS LONG AS YOU'LL BE AT THE MALL ANYWAY, WOULD YOU JUST PICK UP A SUIT FOR ME? BOXER STYLE, 34" WAIST.

SWIMSUIT NO. 1: DOESN'T FIT. WOMAN BLAMES HERSELF. HANGS IT NEATLY BACK ON ITS LITTLE HANGER.

SWIMSUIT NO. 2: DOESN'T FIT. WOMAN PARTIALLY BLAMES HERSELF. PARTIALLY HANGS IT BACK ON ITS LITTLE HANGER.

SWIMSUITS NOS. 3-50: DON'T FIT.
YOU DISGUST ME! YOU REPULSE ME! NO ONE COULD FIT INTO YOU, YOU OVER-PRICED IMPORTS! HAH!
STOMP STOMP
STOMP STOMP

JUST ONCE I WISH THE HUMAN SPIRIT WOULD TRIUMPH IN SOMEONE ELSE'S DEPARTMENT.

THAT DOES IT. I'M BOYCOTTING SWIMSUITS THIS YEAR, MOM.
YOU BOYCOTTED SWIMSUITS LAST YEAR, CATHY.
SWIMWEAR

LOOK WHO'S TALKING. YOU HAVEN'T BOUGHT A NEW SWIMSUIT SINCE 1956.
HA, HA! I GUESS IT RUNS IN THE FAMILY!
SWIMWEAR

WHAT RUNS IN THE FAMILY?
AS OUR FIGURES MATURE, WE KNOW THAT GOOD OLD COVERAGE IS MORE IMPORTANT THAN SOME FLASHY TREND!

WHAT HAVEN'T I TRIED ON YET??
NOTHING BRINGS THEM AROUND LIKE A FEW MINUTES WITH MOM.

MY LEGS LOOK FAT.
MY WAIST LOOKS FAT.
MY ARMS LOOK FAT.

MY KNEES LOOK FAT.
MY ANKLES LOOK FAT.
MY CHIN LOOKS FAT.
MY HAIR LOOKS FAT.
MY EYELIDS LOOK FAT.
MY FEET LOOK FAT.
MY TEETH LOOK FAT.
MY FINGERS LOOK FAT.

INCREDIBLE.

THE ONLY CELL IN MY BODY THAT ISN'T BUSY LOOKING FAT IS THINKING ABOUT WHAT I CAN EAT FOR LUNCH.

$75 FOR THIS SWIMSUIT ?! ARE YOU CRAZY ? ARE YOU OUT OF YOUR MIND ??
SWIM

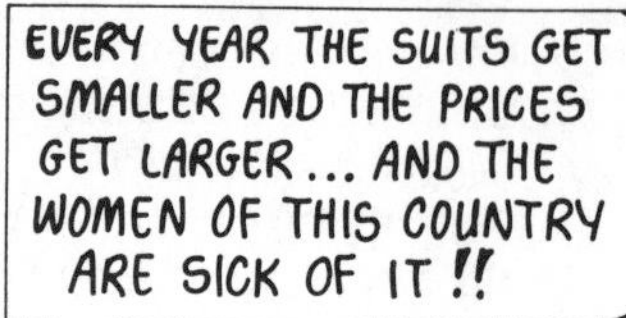
EVERY YEAR THE SUITS GET SMALLER AND THE PRICES GET LARGER ... AND THE WOMEN OF THIS COUNTRY ARE SICK OF IT !!

WE ARE NOT GOING TO TAKE IT ANYMORE ! UNDERSTAND ?? WE ARE NOT GOING TO TAKE IT !

DIDN'T FIT ?
ARE YOU KIDDING ? IF IT HAD FIT, I WOULD HAVE GIVEN HER $300 FOR IT.
SWIMSUITS

WE DO NOT BELIEVE A WOMAN'S WORTH IS MEASURED BY THE SHAPE OF HER BODY !
WE HATE SEXISM ! WE HATE LECHERY !
SWIMWEAR

WE DO NOT BUY SWIMSUITS SO WE CAN "GO ON DISPLAY" !

WE COULD GRAB ANY SUIT ! IT DOES NOT MATTER !!

SWIMWEAR

WE HAVE EVOLVED TO A WHOLE NEW CONSCIOUSNESS !!

SWIMWEAR

... IF I'M GOING TO BE A HYPOCRITE, AT LEAST I WANT TO LOOK CUTE.
WHERE ARE THE ONES WITH THE LITTLE ZIPPERS UP THE FRONT ?
SWIMWEAR

DON'T YOU WANT TO GO TO THE POOL AND TRY OUT YOUR NEW BATHING SUIT, CATHY ?
I CAN'T. I HAVE A HEADACHE.

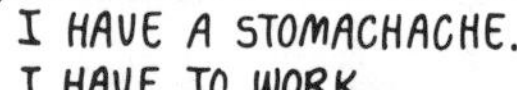
I HAVE A STOMACHACHE.
I HAVE TO WORK.
I HAVE TO DO ERRANDS.
I HAVE TO DO THE LAUNDRY.
I HAVE TO WASH THE CAR.
I HAVE TO CLEAN HOUSE.
I HAVE TO BATHE ELECTRA.
I HAVE TO CALL MY MOTHER.
I HAVE TO BUY GROCERIES.
I HAVE TO PAY BILLS.

ELEVEN LIES IS AS CLOSE TO THE MOMENT OF TRUTH AS I CAN GET FOR THE DAY.

I SPENT HALF AN HOUR TRYING TO DECIDE WHICH FIVE-MINUTE MICROWAVE MEAL TO BUY FOR DINNER...
FROZEN FOODS

I SPENT TWO HOURS TRYING TO FIGURE OUT HOW TO TAPE A 30-MINUTE PROGRAM SO I COULD WATCH IT LATER WHEN I'D HAVE MORE TIME...
VCR VOL. III
VCR VOL. I

I THEN DROVE 40 MINUTES ROUND TRIP TO MY HEALTH CLUB SO I COULD WAIT IN LINE FOR 20 MINUTES TO RIDE A STATIONARY BIKE FOR 10 MINUTES...
Workout

ANOTHER EVENING WIPED OUT BY MODERN CONVENIENCES.
Guisewite

I USED TO COUNT EVERY CALORIE I ATE AND RECORD IT IN A LITTLE BOOK...
LOW-CALORIE DIET

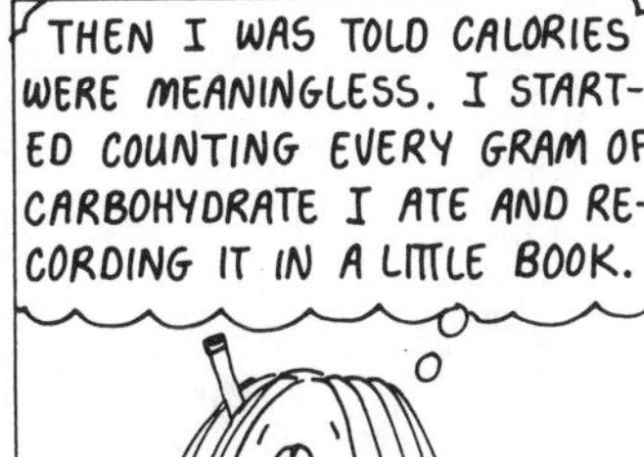
THEN I WAS TOLD CALORIES WERE MEANINGLESS. I STARTED COUNTING EVERY GRAM OF CARBOHYDRATE I ATE AND RECORDING IT IN A LITTLE BOOK.

LOW-CARB. DIET

NOW I'M TOLD CARBOHYDRATES ARE MEANINGLESS. I'VE STARTED COUNTING EVERY GRAM OF FAT I EAT AND RECORDING IT IN A LITTLE BOOK.
LOW-FAT DIET

HOW MANY YEARS MUST I SPIN MY WHEELS BEFORE I GET TO LOSE 10 POUNDS?
Guisewite

THE FISH MUST BE POACHED! NO BREADING!
THE CHICKEN MUST BE BROILED! NO SKIN!

THE BROCCOLI MUST BE STEAMED! NO BUTTER!
THE SALAD MUST BE PLAIN! NO DRESSING!

NO CROUTONS! NO GRATED CHEESE! NO OIL! NO SAUCES!

WOULD YOU CARE TO SEE THE DESSERT CART, OR WILL YOU BE SNEAKING ACROSS THE STREET FOR CHEESECAKE ON THE WAY BACK TO THE OFFICE?

BUTTER?
NO. A PAT OF BUTTER HAS 7 GRAMS OF FAT, WHICH IS 26% OF THE FAT ALLOWED ALL DAY ON MY 30% FAT DIET. SALAD DRESSING?

NO, THANKS. THE HALF-CUP OF AVOCADO IN MY SALAD ALREADY HAS 16.6 GRAMS OF FAT, WHICH, IF ADDED TO THE 14.5 GRAMS OF FAT IN TWO TABLESPOONS OF DRESSING, WOULD NOT EVEN ALLOW ME THE OPTION OF HAVING 2% MILK IN MY COFFEE!

ALL THINGS CONSIDERED, SHOULDN'T ONE OF US BE ABLE TO FIGURE OUT A 15% TIP?

WHAT ARE YOU THINKING ABOUT, CATHY?

I WAS JUST THINKING ABOUT MY FAT CELLS. SINCE THEY INSIST ON LIVING IN MY BODY, I WAS WONDERING IF I COULD CONVINCE THEM TO MOVE TO MY HAIR SO MY HAIR COULD BE NICE AND FULL AND MY BODY COULD FINALLY BE THIN.

OH.

NOTHING KILLS A CONVERSATION LIKE SAYING WHAT'S ON YOUR MIND.

"THE PROPER DIET SHOULD DERIVE NO MORE THAN 30% OF ITS TOTAL CALORIES FROM FAT, WHICH SHOULD BE EQUALLY DISTRIBUTED AMONG POLYUNSATURATED, MONOUNSATURATED AND SATURATED FAT..."
LOW FAT DIET

"IN A 1,500-CALORIE DIET, THIS WOULD BE A MAXIMUM OF 50 GRAMS OF FAT, OR 10 GRAMS MORE OR LESS FOR EACH 300-CALORIE INCREASE OR DECREASE IN TOTAL CALORIC ALLOTMENT, FIGURING 9 CALORIES PER GRAM OF FAT, AND 28 GRAMS PER OUNCE..."
LOW FAT

"AS IN ALL DIETS, SIMPLE COMMON SENSE SHOULD BE YOUR BEST GUIDE."

I WEIGH TWO POUNDS LESS IF THE SCALE IS ON A CARPETED FLOOR.

NO MESSAGES. HOW DO I KNOW IF I MADE IRVING JEALOUS OR NOT IF HE DIDN'T LEAVE A MESSAGE ?

YOU WERE HERE, ELECTRA. DID SOMEONE CALL AND NOT LEAVE A MESSAGE ?? DID SOMEONE HANG UP BEFORE THE BEEP ??

HOW MANY TIMES DID SOME-ONE HANG UP BEFORE THE BEEP ?? DID YOU HEAR HIM BREATHING BEFORE THE HANG UP ?? DID IT SOUND LIKE IRVING ? THINK, ELECTRA !

WHATEVER HAPPENED TO THE GOOD OLD DAYS WHEN ALL A DOG HAD TO DO FOR A COOKIE WAS LEARN TO SIT ?
GUISEWITE

I WILL NOT THINK ABOUT MY NEW FOOD PROGRAM FOR LIFE. I WILL NOT THINK ABOUT NOT THINKING ABOUT MY NEW FOOD PROGRAM FOR LIFE. I WILL NOT THINK ABOUT FOOD, PROGRAMS OR LIFE. I WILL NOT THINK ABOUT NOT THINKING ABOUT **WHAT I AM NOT THINKING ABOUT.**

THE WORKOUT VIDEO IS IN MY HAND. THE VCR IS 12 INCHES AWAY. PUT THE TAPE IN THE MACHINE. JUST MOVE ONE MUSCLE AND PUT THE TAPE IN THE MACHINE. JUST MOVE. MOVE **ANY** MUSCLE. **JUST MOVE ONE MUSCLE.**

THERE'S HALF A CANDY BAR IN THE LEFT POCKET OF A JACKET THAT FELL BEHIND A FILE CABINET, UP TWO FLIGHTS OF STAIRS, 20 MILES AWAY AT THE OFFICE.

WORSE...WORSE...BETTER ...WORSE...BETTER...BETTER ...BETTER...WORSE...BETTER... WORSE...BETTER...WORSE...

...BEGINNING STUDENTS SHOULD REMEMBER TO PACE THEIR GAWKING SO THEY'LL HAVE STRENGTH LEFT FOR WHAT THEY'LL BE SEEING IN THE LOCKER ROOM....

I WORKED OUT BEFORE COMING TO THE OFFICE TODAY! I FEEL FANTASTIC!

CHARLENE

YOU SHOULD WORK OUT, CHARLENE! EVERYONE SHOULD WORK OUT!!

I AM INCORPORATING WORKING OUT INTO EACH AND EVERY DAY! I WILL GO NOWHERE WITHOUT MY WORKOUT GEAR! WORKING OUT IS MY LIFE!

SPLAT!
BAD NEWS, MR. PINKLEY. ANOTHER EMPLOYEE HAS BECOME PHYSICALLY FIT.

WHEN YOU EXERCISE, YOUR BRAIN PRODUCES CHEMICALS THAT KEEP YOU FROM FEELING HUNGRY FOR UP TO SIX HOURS!
YOU'RE RIGHT. I DON'T FEEL HUNGRY, CATHY.
AEROBICS ROOM
SCHEDULE

SEE? WE'RE DRIVING HOME AND I STILL DON'T FEEL HUNGRY!
WE COULD DRIVE RIGHT UP TO A COOKIE STORE AND I WOULDN'T FEEL HUNGRY!

HA, HA! WE COULD GET OUT OF THE CAR AND BREATHE CHOCOLATE CHIP COOKIE AIR AND NOT FEEL HUNGRY!...
...I COULD HOLD A HOT, GOOEY CHOCOLATE CHIP COOKIE IN MY HAND AND NOT FEEL HUNGRY!!

....I FEEL SICK.
WHICH CHEMICAL MUST MY BRAIN PRODUCE BEFORE I LEARN TO NOT RIDE HOME WITH MY DIET BUDDY?...
COOKIES

I WAS PERFECT ON MY WORKOUT PROGRAM AND THEN I GOT BUSY AND HAD TO SKIP ONE DAY...

SINCE I SKIPPED ONE DAY, THE WEEK IS RUINED, AND I MIGHT AS WELL SKIP THE REST OF THE WEEK... SINCE THE WEEK IS RUINED, THE MONTH IS RUINED AND I MIGHT AS WELL SKIP THE REST OF THE MONTH...

SINCE THE MONTH IS RUINED, THE YEAR IS RUINED. SINCE THE YEAR IS RUINED, MY WHOLE TRACK RECORD FOR LIFE IS RUINED...

IN MY NEXT REINCARNATION, I WILL BE PERFECT FROM THE SECOND I'M BORN!

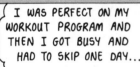

BAD GIRL, ELECTRA! YOU CHEWED UP MY MAIL AGAIN! BAD! BAD! BAD!

...IT'S AN ENGAGEMENT ANNOUNCEMENT FROM JANE! JANE'S ONLY KNOWN HIM FOR SIX MONTHS! HOW CAN JANE BE ENGAGED??!

BLEAH!
RIP RIP RIP RIP RIP
RIP RIP RIP RIP

HUMANS: YOU CAN'T LIVE WITH THEM, YOU CAN'T LIVE WITHOUT THEM.

HOW DID HE PROPOSE, JANE?
OH, IT WAS SO ROMANTIC!

I DROPPED HINTS FOR MONTHS...I BEGGED, WHINED, WHIMPERED, COAXED, SEDUCED, PLOTTED AND SCHEMED....

THEN, FOR MY GRAND FINALE, I STOMPED OUT OF HIS HOUSE SOBBING THAT I NEVER WANTED TO SEE HIS MISERABLE FACE AGAIN....AND HE SAID, WELL, OK, MAYBE WE COULD TRY GETTING ENGAGED!!

VERY ROMANTIC.
TECHNICALLY, THE WORDS CAME OUT OF HIS LIPS.
JUST LIKE IN THE MOVIES!

I WOULD NEVER TRICK A MAN INTO WANTING TO BE WITH ME, CHARLENE.
EXCEPT FOR MAKEUP. IT'S OK TO TRICK HIM A LITTLE BIT WITH MAKEUP.
Flowers

AND CLOTHES. TRICKING HIM WITH CLOTHES IS OK.
ALSO COLOGNE, CANDLELIGHT, ROMANTIC MUSIC, SEXY MOVIES AND ALL HIS FAVORITE FOODS.

IT'S OK TO GET HIM EMOTIONALLY DEPENDENT ON ME FOR ALL THE COZY COMFORTS OF LIFE WHILE SIMULTANEOUSLY LETTING HIM HEAR AN OCCASIONAL PHONY MESSAGE ON MY MACHINE FROM ANOTHER MAN...BUT I WOULD NEVER REALLY TRICK HIM!

SOME WOMEN HAVE NO SELF-RESPECT.
WHAT DO YOU THINK THEY'VE TRIED THAT WE HAVEN'T THOUGHT OF YET?...
Flowers

AFTER $20 BILLION OF RESEARCH, NUCLEAR FUSION HAS JUST BEEN CREATED BY TWO WOMEN AND A COPY OF COSMOPOLITAN MAGAZINE.

I INVITED IRVING TO DINNER IN THE MOST EXPENSIVE RESTAURANT IN TOWN SO I COULD PROPOSE... JUST LIKE YOU SUGGESTED!
YOU'RE KIDDING. YOU'RE GOING THROUGH WITH IT?!

YOU TOLD ME THAT, DEEP DOWN, HE WANTED ME TO PROPOSE... THAT WE BOTH NEEDED THE EMOTIONAL LIBERATION OF A PROPOSAL!!
I DIDN'T THINK YOU'D ACTUALLY DO IT!

CHARLENE, YOU SPENT FIVE HOURS TALKING ME INTO THIS!! THE WHEELS ARE IN MOTION!!!
HA, HA! WELL, GOOD LUCK! WANT A FROZEN YOGURT OR SOMETHING?

NEVER UNDERESTIMATE THE HIGH PRICE OF A CHEAP THERAPIST.

THIS IS THE NIGHT I PROPOSE TO IRVING. MY SWEETIE. THE LOVE OF MY LIFE.

ISN'T THAT CUTE? HE'S DOING THAT FUNNY THING WITH HIS DINNER ROLL. THAT FUNNY THING THAT I HATE. HA, HA. NO. NOT HATE. I ADORE HIS FUNNY LITTLE REPULSIVE HABITS.

NOW HE'S PICKING ALL THE TOMATOES OUT OF HIS SALAD. **I HATE WHEN HE PICKS TOMATOES OUT OF HIS SALAD.** NO. HE'S MY SWEETIE. I LOVE **EVERYTHING** HE DOES. **EXCEPT THAT.** EXCEPT WHEN HE CLINKS HIS SPOON LIKE THAT. **NO.** CLINKING IS FINE. **SO WHAT IF I HAVE TO LISTEN TO THAT CLINKING SPOON FOR THE WHOLE REST OF MY-**

AACK!
JUST ONCE I WISH THEY'D HAVE THEIR REVELATIONS AFTER I GOT MY TIP.

DO WE HAVE TO LISTEN TO THIS MUSIC, IRVING?
WE ALWAYS LISTEN TO THIS MUSIC, CATHY.

WE ALWAYS LISTEN TO THIS MUSIC BECAUSE YOU ALWAYS PLAY THIS MUSIC.
IF YOU DON'T LIKE THIS MUSIC, WHY DON'T YOU PLAY DIFFERENT MUSIC?

BECAUSE I'D RATHER LISTEN TO MUSIC I HATE AND KNOW YOU'RE HAPPY THAN LISTEN TO MUSIC I LOVE AND THINK YOU MIGHT NOT LIKE IT. FOR ONCE YOU COULD APPRECIATE THAT AND CHANGE THE TAPE ON YOUR OWN!!

WHY DO I ALWAYS WIND UP GETTING PUNISHED FOR THE NICE THINGS SHE DOES FOR ME?

WHEN YOUR FRIENDS HAVE CHILDREN, NOTHING CHANGES BETWEEN YOU, IRVING.

WHEN MY FRIENDS HAVE CHILDREN, THE WHOLE FRIENDSHIP DETERIORATES. WE DON'T EVEN SPEAK THE SAME LANGUAGE ANYMORE!

MEN DON'T KNOW WHAT IT'S LIKE TO BE SO CLOSE TO SOMEONE AND HAVE SOME LITTLE BABY COME BETWEEN THEM, DO THEY, ELECTRA? NO!

N-O-O-O-O...MEN JUST DON'T KNOW, DO THEY, MY SNUGGLY LITTLE CUPCAKE???

MEN GET A HINT NOW AND THEN.

FROM THE SECOND I DECIDED TO ASK IRVING TO MARRY ME, I HAVEN'T BEEN ABLE TO STAND BEING IN THE SAME ROOM WITH HIM.

EVERYTHING ABOUT HIM ANNOYS ME. I DON'T LIKE HIS HAIR. I CAN'T STAND HIS CLOTHES. HIS STORIES GIVE ME A HEADACHE AND HIS LAUGH MAKES MY SKIN ITCH.

CATHY, RELAX. YOU HAVE SOMETHING **RIGHT NOW** WITH IRVING THAT PEOPLE SPEND THEIR WHOLE LIVES SEARCHING FOR...

PERSPECTIVE.
AACK! NOT THAT!!
LEAVE IT TO A MARRIED WOMAN TO TAKE THE ROMANCE OUT OF DISILLUSIONMENT.

IRVING'S ALWAYS PUT HIS OWN INTERESTS AND SCHEDULE BEFORE YOURS, CATHY.
I THOUGHT HE WAS JUST GIVING ME SPACE.

HE'S DONE EVERYTHING POSSIBLE TO AVOID ANY BIG COMMITMENT.
I THOUGHT HE WAS JUST BEING COY.

HE'S BEHAVED EXACTLY THE SAME SINCE THE DAY YOU MET... WHAT GROUNDS DO YOU HAVE TO CRITICIZE HIM **NOW**?

YOU AREN'T THE PERSON I WAS PRETENDING YOU WERE!!

WHEN SOMETHING WONDERFUL HAPPENS WITH IRVING, SHE RUNS TO TELL HER MOTHER.

WHEN SOMETHING HORRIBLE HAPPENS, SHE RUNS TO TELL HER MOTHER.

THE WHOLE REST OF THE TIME--INCLUDING ALL MOMENTS LEADING UP TO THE WONDERFUL OR HORRIBLE EVENTS--SHE DOESN'T SAY A PEEP.

MOTHERHOOD: ALL HEADLINES, NO TEXT.

I DON'T THINK WE SHOULD SEE EACH OTHER ANYMORE.

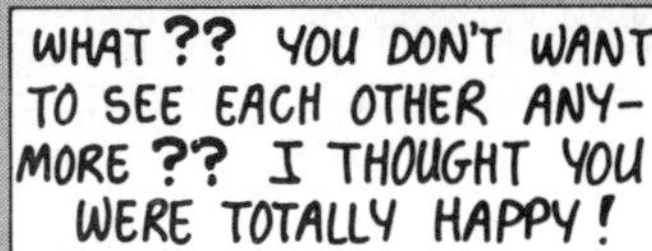
WHAT?? YOU DON'T WANT TO SEE EACH OTHER ANYMORE?? I THOUGHT YOU WERE TOTALLY HAPPY!

WHEN DID YOU DECIDE WE SHOULDN'T SEE EACH OTHER ANYMORE?? I CAN'T BELIEVE IT! WHEN WERE YOU GOING TO SPRING THIS ONE ON ME?!!

AT LAST. PERFECT HARMONY.

I CAN'T BELIEVE I WAS PLANNING TO PROPOSE TO YOU. YOU MAKE ME SICK!
YOU REPULSE ME!

YOU DISGUST ME!
YOU LIVE IN FANTASY LAND!
HAH! I'M THE ONLY LINK TO REALITY THIS RELATIONSHIP EVER HAD!
HAH!

SLAM!

...WHAT WOULD YOUR ANSWER HAVE BEEN?

YOU'RE NEVER SEEING IRVING AGAIN?
NEVER. EXCEPT HE HAS TO GET HIS STUFF FROM MY HOUSE AND I HAVE TO GET MY STUFF FROM HIS HOUSE.

AFTER THAT YOU'RE NEVER SEEING HIM AGAIN?
NEVER. EXCEPT HE HAS TO COME OVER AND FIX THE STEREO HE SMASHED WHEN WE HAD OUR LAST FIGHT.

AFTER THAT?
NEVER. EXCEPT I HAVE TO GIVE HIM RIDES UNTIL HIS CAR GETS BUMPED OUT FROM WHEN I ACCIDENTALLY THREW HIS GOLF CLUBS AT IT.

YOU'RE A ROCK, CATHY.
NOW THAT WE'VE BROKEN UP, I'M SEEING HIM SEVEN NIGHTS A WEEK.

IF THE BREAKUP WAS ALL HIS IDEA, I'D SCREAM, CRY AND HUMILIATE MYSELF BY WRITING DESPERATE LETTERS BEGGING TO HAVE HIM BACK.

IF THE BREAKUP WAS ALL MY IDEA, I'D STOMP AROUND RECITING HIS FLAWS AND BRIBE FRIENDS TO SPY ON HIM AND TELL ME HOW MISERABLE HE WAS.

THE BREAKUP WAS MUTUAL. NO ONE'S FAULT. BOTH SIDES TOTALLY AGREED.

I'VE BEEN ROBBED OF MY WHOLE REPERTOIRE!

YOU'RE NOT UPSET THAT IRVING AND I BROKE UP?
OH, CATHY, ALL THAT MATTERS IS THAT YOU'RE HAPPY.

I'VE ENJOYED GETTING TO KNOW IRVING OVER THE YEARS... BUT I'M JUST YOUR MOTHER! ONLY YOU KNOW WHAT'S RIGHT FOR YOU!

THANKS, MOM. THAT REALLY HELPS.

I HAVE TO START ALL OVER AGAIN!!

I WILL NOT CALL IRVING. WE'VE BROKEN UP. I HAD MY REASONS. GOOD REASONS.

CONCENTRATE ON THE REASONS. THINK OF ALL THE BAD TIMES. FOCUS ON THE HIDEOUS TIMES. ENUMERATE HIS FLAWS.

VISUALIZE HIM AT HIS WORST. DWELL ON EVERY NEGATIVE PERSONALITY TRAIT. DREDGE UP EACH AND EVERY ICKY ENCOUNTER AND FEEL IT FOR THE FIRST TIME ALL OVER AGAIN....

...ANOTHER WILD AND CRAZY SATURDAY NIGHT, SEARCHING FOR NEW WAYS TO KEEP THE BREAKUP FRESH.

BREAKING UP NOT ONLY FREES US TO BE **WITH** SOMEONE ELSE, BUT ALSO FREES US TO **BECOME** SOMEONE ELSE...

WHILE WE ALL FEEL THE SAME POWERFUL URGE TO RENEW WHO WE ARE... OVER THE YEARS, EACH SEX HAS FOUND ITS OWN SPECIAL WAY OF LIVING IT OUT....

MEN DRIVE FLASHY RED SPORTS CARS...

...WOMEN WEAR THEM ON OUR HEADS.

AACK! YOU TURNED MY HAIR **ORANGE!!**

RED. AND BESIDES, IT'LL TONE DOWN IN A COUPLE OF WEEKS.

SALON

MY HAIR IS BRIGHT ORANGE!
NONSENSE. THE RINSE JUST BROUGHT OUT YOUR NATURAL HIGHLIGHTS!
SALON

JUST MAKE SURE YOU LET IT SET OVERNIGHT.
I'M SUPPOSED TO LET IT SET OVERNIGHT ?

OH, YES! YOU'D HATE TO HAVE SPENT $125 ON THIS BEAUTIFUL COLOR AND THEN RISK WASHING IT OUT THE FIRST DAY!
SALO
SALON

SHAMPOO

HI, CHARLENE. IT'S CATHY. PLEASE TELL MR. PINKLEY I WON'T BE IN TODAY.
RECEPTIONIST

I'M NOT FEELING WELL. THERE'S A FAMILY EMERGENCY. MY CAR BROKE DOWN AND ELECTRA HAS AN IMPORTANT DOCTOR'S APPOINTMENT.

RECEPTIONIST

WHAT COLOR IS YOUR HAIR ?
RECEPTIONIST

HOW DID YOU KNOW ?
FROM THE CRACKLE IN YOUR VOICE, I'D SAY IT'S BRIGHT ORANGE.

IT SAYS TO TEST A STRAND OF HAIR FIRST.
I'VE DONE THIS A MILLION TIMES, CATHY!
INSTRUCTIONS

IT SAYS NOT TO USE ON HAIR THAT'S ALREADY BEEN COLORED ORANGE.
THEY'RE JUST BEING OVER-PROTECTIVE!
INSTRUCTIONS

TRUST ME! I JUST SLATHER ON SOME TINT... WAIT A WHILE.. POP OFF THE LITTLE CAP AND...

AAACK!
MAY I ASSUME I DON'T LOOK LIKE THE WOMAN ON THE BOX?

I DEMAND TO SEE THE DRUG ADDICT WHO DYED MY HAIR ORANGE!!

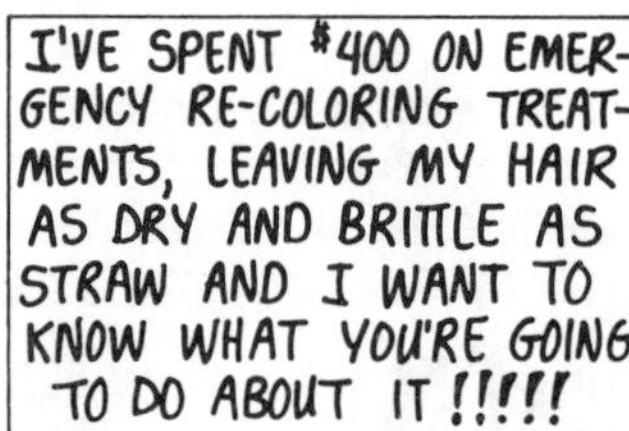
I'VE SPENT $400 ON EMERGENCY RE-COLORING TREATMENTS, LEAVING MY HAIR AS DRY AND BRITTLE AS STRAW AND I WANT TO KNOW WHAT YOU'RE GOING TO DO ABOUT IT!!!!!

SALON

HOW ABOUT A NICE "SUMMER BLONDE" RINSE? ONLY $95.
OK.
SALON

...HOPE: YOU CAN BREAK OFF ALL THE ENDS, BUT YOU CAN'T KILL THE ROOTS.

CATHY, IT'S IRVING. I NEED TO SEE YOU.
COOKIES

I CAN'T SEE YOU ANYMORE, IRVING. I'VE CHANGED.
I KNOW YOU'VE CHANGED... BUT I'VE CHANGED, TOO.

I'VE GOTTEN WORSE.
COOKIES

DO YOU THINK YOU'LL EVER HAVE A BABY, CATHY ?
YAP YAP YAP YAP
BAM BAM BAM

I HOPE SO, ANDREA. DO YOU THINK YOU'LL EVER GET A DOG ?
I HOPE SO.
YAP YAP YAP YAP
BAM BAM BAM

THERE'S NOTHING LIKE SEEING SOME-ONE ELSE'S LITTLE ONE TO REAFFIRM THAT OLD FEELING...
YEAH...

MINE WILL BE DIFFERENT....
YAP YAP YAP YAP YAP YAP
BAM BAM BAM BAM BAM
Guisewite